PRACTICAL TIPS TO GET YOU EATING REAL FOODS AGAIN

Zoe and I would like to thank you for purchasing this book and helping
us to spread its message into the community. We will be donating 15 per cent
of the profits to the Mai Wiru Sugar Challenge Foundation
and to the That Sugar Film Schools Program.

Please visit **maiwirufoundation.org** and **thatsugarfilm.com**
for more information and connect about the book on Instagram
and Twitter at **#thatsugarguide**.

THAT Sugar GUIDE

DAMON & ZOE GAMEAU

Pan Macmillan Australia

CONTENTS

The body does not need added sugar. There is no nutritional value to it and there is actually no biological requirement for it by the body.

– DR ASEEM MALHOTRA, UK CARDIOLOGIST

But a little bit every now and then certainly isn't going to hurt.

– DAMON AND ZOE

ANOTHER BOOK?

People occasionally ask me where the name for *That Sugar Film* came from. I'd loosely called the project this from the beginning, but just before we completed the film, some alternative ideas were sent back and forth in a game of email tennis. We bandied around (almost) witty puns like 'Sickly Sweet' and 'Sugar Rush', and cringe-worthy taglines such as 'The bitter truth about sugar' and 'A savoury look at the world of sweet'. I am deeply sorry for ever thinking the last one was okay.

We ended up sticking with *That Sugar Film* for a few reasons. Firstly, I liked the idea that someone scanning the movie section of the newspaper would know in an instant exactly what our film was about.

Secondly, I enjoyed imagining the awkward conversations that our film might be responsible for, but that we would never witness:

'What film are you seeing?' says one.

'Oh, just *That Sugar Film*,' says the other.

'Oh yeah, what's it called?'

But mostly I pondered about high-ranking executives at food companies lamenting their plummeting profits if our film became a box-office hit: '*That Sugar Film*!' would be the cry reverberating down their newly emptied corridors.

What I didn't expect was that the words 'That Sugar ...' would prove to be extremely handy and would later lend themselves to not just a film, but also a book, a free app, a study guide for schools and teachers, a song, and now the carefully constructed former tree you hold in your hands.

What's more, this book is probably the least likely chapter of my life. Five years ago, if you had told me I would make a film and write a book about sugar, I would have scoffed and reached for my can of vanilla-flavoured Coke. But if you had then told me I would go on to write a recipe book packed with practical tips and advice about lowering your sugar intake, I would have shaken that can, pulled the aluminium trigger, and sprayed you with 9 teaspoons of cleverly marketed bumper-bar rust cleaner.

So why another book? Well, this one – a collaboration with my radiant and talented girlfriend, Zoe – came about as a result of the film, specifically the 83 question-and-answer sessions that followed screenings throughout Australia, New Zealand, the UK and USA. These Q&As featured some terrific guest panellists including dieticians, surgeons, town mayors, sports scientists, sugar scientists, nutritionists, AFL footballers, schoolchildren and even Margaret Fulton's granddaughter Kate Gibbs (who has revealed that in the 1960s her grandmother was asked by the Australian Government to double the amount of sugar in her dessert recipes to prop up our sugar industry — strangely enough, I have yet to receive a similar request for this book).

Because what all 83 of these half-hour talkathons revealed was that a) citizens of Earth are wonderful people who are very passionate about their health and their children's future, b) the question 'Can I still drink alcohol?' was asked at every single one of the Australian and New Zealand events, thus revealing a hell of a lot about antipodean culture, and c) people loved being awoken to the information in the film but then wanted practical advice about what to do and what to eat moving forward.

So that's the purpose of this book (plus we also need to raise more money for the Aboriginal Mai Wiru Sugar Challenge Foundation). Within these pages, we will take you through some of the topics that came up during these sessions: questions like 'How do I make sense of food labels?', 'What's the story with artificial sweeteners?' and 'What do I eat when I'm out?' There's also plenty of practical advice about shopping for real foods without breaking the bank, packing healthy lunchboxes for the kids, helping those you love without being a nag, and being kind to yourself during the transition off high-sugar foods. And of course the answer to the booze question (yes, you can, so read no further if you don't want to). Our hope is that when you've finished this book, you will be equipped to dominate any sugar-themed quiz night at the local pub.

Most importantly, we also share the recipes that Zoe nourished me with after my sugar-eating madness had finally ended. Now let's clear something up straight from the get-go: This is not a diet book.

This is a book filled with 80 delicious real-food recipes that we hope will help improve your health and wellbeing. (Just to remind you, at the end of the sugar-eating experiment, I had full-blown fatty liver disease, pre type 2 diabetes, heart-disease risks and 10 centimetres of fructose-induced visceral fat around my belly, and I was 8.5 kilograms overweight.) These meals took me to full health again in just 60 days.

'This is not a diet book.'

Zoe and I have kept the recipes very simple. There is nothing in this book that can't be bought at a large supermarket. There's no Himalayan yak chi powder, organic Alaskan urchin broth or Nordic goat's testicles dipped in goji cacao butter. All the ingredients can be found in shops outside the affluent suburbs of urban Australia where many people have already grasped the low-sugar message. This book is designed to penetrate what I like to call the 'Quinoa Curtain' (although 'Kale Curtain' could also work? 'Kombucha Curtain' may be a bit wordy).

It's important to note that this approach may not work for everyone in the same way it did for me. Science is increasingly telling us that we all respond to foods differently, depending on factors such as hormones, genetics, metabolic health, exercise levels and the world of our individual 'microbiome' (good and bad bacteria). Even the opioid receptors in our brains, which determine our sugar cravings, vary in size. Make sure you see a professional if you are having recurring health problems. They will help tailor a way of eating that suits your particular body type (although I guarantee they won't recommend upping your refined-sugar intake).

Caveats aside, I know from the response to *That Sugar Film* and our previous book that a heart-warming number of people have benefited from reducing their sugar intake. Zoe and I have written this follow-up in the hope that it will help many, many more. Please let us know how you go. We have included interactive sections where you can take photos of your creations and share them with us online so that other people can also be motivated and inspired. We are up against a mightily powerful food industry that has hijacked our understanding of what food really is. It is going to take a combined effort from all of us to influence the future health of our families and friends, so we encourage you to get involved.

On the surface, this book may appear to some as a 'sugar removal' plan (perhaps 'I *almost* Quit Sugar'?). However, I'll let you in on a little secret: it is really just a helpful manual to get you and your family eating and enjoying real foods again. My hope is that one day consuming less sugar will not be thought of as a diet or even a meal plan but will simply be known as *eating*.

'My hope is that one day consuming less sugar will not be thought of as a diet or even a meal plan but will simply be known as *eating*.'

the BRIDGING WEEK

This is the first week of lowering your sugar intake. It can be challenging for some people, so to make the transition easier the Bridging Week recipes still contain an element of sweetness from ingredients such as fruits and coconut. There are 21 recipes to choose from – a week's worth of breakfasts, lunches and dinners.

the CONSOLIDATION PHASE

Once you've completed the Bridging Week, you can move on to the Consolidation Phase. These recipes include many of the meals I ate for the 60 days straight after my high-sugar experiment. They are designed to keep insulin down so you can improve metabolic health, introduce stability to your moods, burn off fat if you would like to and, most importantly, satiate you with proteins and healthy fats so you can resist any cravings that may drop around for a visit.

The Consolidation Phase also includes recipes for school lunch boxes, special treats and snacks, and for when you are feeling happy with your health again and can reintroduce the odd whole grain (no, we don't fear them entirely; see page 49 for an explanation). Our recipes are just a guide and we encourage you to build your own meals using the ingredients list on page 105. Scattered throughout are brief explanations of why we recommend something, with the science to back it up.

We also had a great time devising this menu key, which tells you if something is veggie or vegan, and offers an alternative use for it (like pureed baby food or a next-day lunch, or perhaps a health-conscious food fight).

VEGETARIAN

VEGAN

BABY FRIENDLY

TODDLER FRIENDLY

LEFTOVERS

OCCASIONAL FOODS

WHAT HAPPENS WHEN
YOU REDUCE SUGAR

So perhaps you've been nagged by a friend or your other half about this topic for over a year now. You've finally agreed to at least flick through 'the bloody book' and here you are. Welcome. This chapter will help you understand what happens to your body once you drop the clutch and change down a gear on your sugar consumption. I think the best way to introduce this section and to explain it clearly is to play the analogy game. For the next few paragraphs of carefully assembled letters, we are going to pretend your body is a car.

Step one is to imagine that for most of your life you have been driving a car with the wrong petrol in it (eating a high-sugar diet). Chances are your car needs regular check-ups at the mechanic (doctor). There might be a blocked fuel hose (arteries), a filter that needs replacing (liver or kidneys) or the exhaust pipe may need some propping up (if you read *That Sugar Book* you'll know my testosterone plummeted during the experiment).

The mechanic may help your car by giving you some additives for the engine (medications), just to keep the ole girl running smoothly – and there's no doubt the constant costly trips to the mechanic are having an impact on the holiday fund. (By the way, some mechanics get bonuses for selling you those additives, but that's a whole other story.)

Now imagine you got dragged to the movies one night and saw something called *That Petrol Film*. You had your eyes opened to a few things about engine maintenance and what the service stations get up to. You come home, gather the family in the lounge room and boldly declare: 'From now on, our car is going to run on new fuel.'

And here (finally) is the point. As you head down to the new petrol station (the real-food aisles at the supermarket or maybe the local farmer's market), where you'll fill up your car with the type of petrol it is supposed to run on (real food), it's important to understand there are going to be a

YOUR CAR WILL RUN
BEST WHEN YOU GIVE
IT THE RIGHT FUEL.

few awkward moments while the car gets used to this new fuel. Your car
has been so accustomed to running on different fuel that it may cough and
splutter at the beginning, take a while to get going in the mornings, blare
its horn at random moments and generally feel sluggish, like it has a flat
battery. Yet slowly but surely, with persistence, patience and the right fuel,
the filter will right itself, the pistons will start firing again, the lights will
come on in high beam, the radio will blare with subwoofer bass power and
the newly efficient ole girl will be taking you wherever you want to go.

Basically, in a much more direct way (and if I hadn't been an actor for
12 years), the introduction to this section would read: When you stop
eating so much added sugar and start to fuel yourself with real foods,
your body may need a little time to adjust.

For those more scientifically minded and less into car metaphors, this is for you:

A study at Princeton University in the early 2000s showed that sugar withdrawal was very real in an experiment involving rats. When their sugary goods were removed, the poor rodents suffered from chattering teeth, paw tremors and headshaking. Now to me that sounds like some seriously strung-out rats – somebody please get those rodent dudes a little caramel cheese and a warm blanket. Other studies have shown rats feverishly prodding a lever that releases sugary water and not being anywhere near as determined to get at other substances. What this tells me is that there may be a small hole in a wall somewhere that houses weekly Sugarholics Anonymous Mouse meetings. I can picture groups of mice hanging around outside the hole, smoking tiny cigarettes before they go in.

These sugar withdrawals and cravings aren't just confined to rodents. I certainly had a few such moments when my experiment ended and I segued back to my normal diet. My own 'feverish lever prodding' was thinking about ramming a straw into an UP&GO and getting a sweet hit from its tax-exempt cardboard housing. Judging by the feedback on our social media channels, a substantial number of people (and mice) also relate to this.

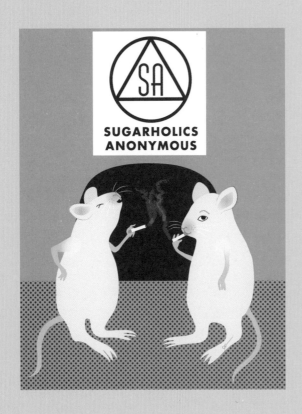

SUGAR WITHDRAWAL
AND COPING WITH CRAVINGS

What helps to shed some light on all of this is understanding that we have evolved to like the taste of sweet foods. It all comes down to a neural pathway in the brain known as the mesolimbic, or reward, pathway.

You see, way back in our formative years as a species, when sonnets were recited in differently accented grunts, we were highly attuned to taste as a way of communicating. Sour tastes told us one thing, perhaps that something wasn't ripe just yet, while bitter tastes often signalled something to perhaps avoid. Sweet tastes, however, lit up this reward pathway in orgiastic celebration and exclaimed, 'Eat this, grunter, because it's high in energy and you need it!'

Of course, when our species was evolving, this signalling was incredibly handy. The sweet taste was stumbled upon very rarely, in seasonal fruit or a beehive (if you had the courage to reach in and steal from our tiny winged and oddly furry friends). But this sweet hit can now be found in nearly 80 per cent of our food. It lurks at every corner shop, supermarket, cafe and school canteen. What hope do most of us have when our mesolimbic pathway is constantly being triggered, lighting the way towards a kingdom of sweet?

The chemicals in our brain responsible for this 'sugar longing' are known as dopamine and opioids. It turns out we all have different-sized receptors for these chemicals and this is why some people crave sugar or feel sugar withdrawals more intensely than others (this also applies to alcohol, cigarettes, drugs and sex). Some people who have eaten a high-sugar diet for many years can actually build up a tolerance, which means they need increasingly more sugar to feel the 'sugar high' or opioid release.

When I interviewed actor and walking Wikipedia Stephen Fry, he mentioned how he had a real desire for sweet food as a child but his siblings could take it or leave it. This is why those who don't experience sugar addiction find it very hard to understand and those who have the addiction struggle to see why people might think they're weirdos. By the way, I am firmly in the Stephen Fry/weirdo camp: Zoe knows not to buy chocolate under 75 per cent cocoa because by morning all that would remain would be slivers of an alfoil wrapper.

GOOGLE 'MONELL CHEMICAL SENSES CENTER' TO LEARN MORE.

ONE OF THE FIRST OF ITS KIND, A 2015 STUDY LOOKED AT HOW QUICKLY CRAVINGS DISAPPEARED AFTER CUTTING OUT SUGAR. FIFTY-THREE PER CENT OF PARTICIPANTS LOST THEIR SUGAR CRAVINGS AFTER THREE DAYS, AND 86 PER CENT AFTER SIX DAYS.

What all this means is that for some people, lowering sugar intake can be very tough, while others will feel fine and not understand what all the fuss is about. We are all different. If you suspect it might be a bit tricky for you, here's some comforting advice that made a world of difference to me and helped with the cravings early on:

Eat a Snickers!

Apologies – that's what the voice in my head was saying. I suggest listening to a really smart scientist instead:

A study by Dr Eric Stice and his team at the Oregon Research Institute revealed that, like sugar, fat activates reward centres in the brain, albeit at a slightly lower strength. Which means that eating some healthy fat – a spoonful of avocado or coconut, for example – can be a big help if you're finding it difficult to shake a craving. (My current favourite is toasted coconut flakes with no added sugar. Wowsers, they're good.) You could also try one of Zoe's smoothies on pages 162–63.

Or you could follow the advice of a nutritionist I met in the USA, who told me to use reverse psychology on cravings by swigging something foul like apple cider vinegar – your brain will be reluctant to send the craving signal if all you keep giving it is face-contorting tonic.

THE LIVER: EMPLOYEE OF THE MONTH

While the mental effects of sugar withdrawal may leave you feeling like you've been smacked in the face with a Coke vending machine, your body will also go through its own set of adjustments. Just to recap, during my high-sugar experiment, I put on 8.5 kilos, developed a fatty liver, showed early signs of type 2 diabetes and heart-disease risks, gained 10 cm of visceral fat around my belly, plus stubbed my toe (it happened early one morning when I was grumpy and racing to the fridge for a Ribena, so I blame sugar).

But the biggest surprise to all of us working on *That Sugar Film* was the remarkable thing that happened to my body once I lowered my sugar intake again and returned to the foods that you are clearly interested in if you've bought this book.

Although every organ is vital to our finely tuned system, if there was an 'Employee of the month' award handed out to body parts, then the liver would have a pool-room wall to boast about. The liver is the largest organ in the body and its impressive resume includes duties very relevant to our conversation. Among other things, it:

» removes toxins;
» processes nutrients;
» helps to regulate metabolism;
» and deals with fat accumulation.

EMPLOYEE
OF THE MONTH

AWARDED TO

LIVER

JANUARY

EMPLOYEE
OF THE MONTH

AWARDED TO

LIVER

FEBRUARY

EMPLOYEE
OF THE MONTH

AWARDED TO

LIVER

MARCH

EMPLOYEE
OF THE MONTH

AWARDED TO

PANCREAS

APRIL

★ LIVER ★
RESUME
PERSONAL SKILLS

- removes toxins
- processes nutrients
- helps to regulate metabolism
- deals with fat accumulation

The delightful fatty-liver disease I acquired during the high-sugar experiment came about because of the unique way fructose metabolises in the body. (Remember sugar is sucrose, which is made up of 50 per cent glucose and 50 per cent fructose.) Fructose turns to fat in the liver. And when you know the other functions of the liver, it is clear that any damage it sustains has a substantial knock-on effect. Turning my liver to fat affected my ability to clear and remove toxins from my body, and it interfered with the regulation of my metabolism – to the point that I became insulin sensitive, doubled my production of insulin and ended up being pre type 2 diabetes. And when excess insulin is in the blood, not only does it dabble in type 2 diabetes, it also tells fat to stay in the fat cells: it turns off our fat-burning processes.

But before you purse your lips and say, 'Well, this is only your story, an experiment of N=1', not only do I say you are correct, smarty-pants, but I point you to the growing prevalence of my symptoms in the population (nearly 6 million Australians now have non-alcoholic fatty liver disease and it didn't exist 35 years ago), plus I throw a wad of science at you.

My results directly mirror many studies around the world including those by Dr Kimber Stanhope at University of California, Davis. (Kimber is also involved with the terrific website Sugar Science.org, which has reviewed more than 8000 papers linking sugar and disease.) Dr Stanhope and her fructose detectives showed that human guinea pigs eating a fructose diet developed increased fatty liver, increased lipid risk factors (fat in the blood) and a 17 per cent change in insulin sensitivity when compared to a group eating the same amount of calories from glucose – meaning steps were taken firmly in the direction of fatty liver disease, type 2 diabetes and heart disease. (More studies have recently emerged showing very similar results to mine and they are listed neatly on page 230.)

I think we need to head back to the garage now and tune the radio station from 'The Science Show' to 'Easy Listening Metaphors'. What all this equates to is that your health relies heavily on your liver functioning like a Formula 1 car. You are the pit crew in charge of maintenance and after seeing *That Petrol Film* you know that your car needs the right fuel to have the best chance of winning the race. And here's the tip: that fuel ain't sugar.

Water is that fuel. I completely turned around my fatty liver disease, in just 60 days by eliminating the sugar and by drinking water. I treated my liver as you would a toddler. Drinking water was like running it a daily bath; I gently cleaned behind its ears, calmly

'I treated my liver as you would a toddler. I gently cleaned behind its ears, calmly dealt with its ablutions and thought seriously about reading it a bedtime story.'

ONCE UPON A TIME THERE WAS
A MOLECULE CALLED FRUCTOSE.

dealt with its ablutions and thought seriously about reading it a bedtime story, but realised that would have been tough to explain if I was caught.

The water worked. All my blood tests returned to normal and the flow-on effect was enormous. No more fatty liver, no more pre type 2 diabetes, no more heart-disease risks, and 90 per cent of the gained weight gone: all from reducing the amount of refined white crystals I poured into my face cave. Especially the ones that come in liquid form.

Caveat time again: not everyone will be able to completely reverse their symptoms. However, by eating real foods and lowering your sugar intake you will be catapulting your body in the right direction.

PALADJUSTMENT:
A HALLELUJAH MOMENT

Another joy of doing 83 Q&As with the film (and, believe me, repeatedly being subjected to the last two minutes of the song at the end of the film wasn't one) was that the audience shared their own stories of life with less sugar. Many women told me how this new way of eating had helped their PCOS (Polycystic Ovary Syndrome), improved sleeping patterns or balanced their children's moods. Others reported alleviated symptoms of asthma, muscle pain, arthritis and skin disorders. The general consensus was that life dramatically improved in some way when the sweet gear was consumed as it was always intended – as an occasional treat.

Strong scientific evidence now supports the link between sugar and inflammation, which is instrumental in many of the above conditions. It is estimated that around 70 per cent of our immune cells are in our digestive system. This means these cells interact with and are affected by the foods we eat. Highly processed and sugary foods will take you down one path, while nourishing, real foods will take you down a different one. A study in the *American Journal of Clinical Nutrition* reported that refined sugars and refined carbohydrates (such as white-flour foods) can increase inflammation, which can cause pain, overheating, redness and swelling. This gives white-lab-coated support to many of the tales I heard on the

> '**When you step away from excess sugar, you will start to notice the subtle flavours of real and natural foods again.**'

Q&A tour and is the reason you will find none of those foods in our book. Indeed, many of our recipes are ideal for helping curb inflammation. Purple cabbage and dark-green veggies are rich in vitamin C and other antioxidants that dampen inflammation; cruciferous vegetables such as broccoli, cauliflower, brussels sprouts and kale are also terrific.

But if the veggie list I just reeled off makes you feel gut-wrenchingly depressed and you're worried your life with less sugar will be nothing more than eating bland vegetables and dried seaweed sheets, fear not. The most significant change you will experience through the whole process is your palate adjustment, or the more scientific term 'paladjustment', which is a word I have just, in this moment, invented.

Paladjustment means that when you step away from excess sugar, you will start to notice the subtle flavours of natural foods again. When your mouth is not being nuclear-bombed 35 times a day with a refined, chemically bleached crystal that makes for an effective scrubbing agent, other tastes actually get a look in. I was a man who loved and drank two vanilla-flavoured Cokes each day for 15 years, yet now a banana is almost too sweet for me. 'What a load of hippy dippy bullshit,' I would've told you five years ago. Well, my friends, it isn't. To me now, a sip of vanilla-flavoured Coke is akin to licking the chlorinated filter at a tiny tots' swimming centre: sensorially overwhelming and tasting suspiciously like piss.

The paladjustment I speak of is a hallelujah moment for most people and you won't understand it until you have experienced it for yourself. Most of us have consumed added sugar in some form – hidden in sauce or yoghurt or juice or cereal or soup or bread or ham or baby food or mayonnaise or baked beans – every day since childhood. It is only when you remove it that you will finally understand what all the (slightly mad and sometimes frustrating) 'sugar fanatics' have been banging on about. I urge you to give it a try and then join the army; the children of the future need you in their fight for health and wellness.

I would now like to hand over the writing reins to Zoe. Here is some wonderful advice that really helped me after my experiment – all delivered with a considered, more nurturing, 'bed of feathery pillows' approach . . .

#paladjustment

Zoe *the* EMOTIONAL ELEMENT

Before Damon had started the editing process for the film, he showed me a clip, an interview with the wonderful Dr Kathleen DesMaisons. Her heartfelt sentiments on the effects of sugar moved me deeply, and I felt she was a powerful voice for so many who struggle with it. This quote, especially, stuck with me: 'Sugar releases the same opioids in the brain as love does. That's why breaking up with sugar can be very difficult for some people.'

So, as you make this transition, it is essential to treat yourself with loving kindness. You are taking active and conscious steps towards improving your health. It is important to match your thinking and self-talk to the positive changes you are undergoing physically.

If you have relied on sugar or unknowingly sugar-laden foods as your regular source of comfort, you will undoubtedly miss some of these old familiars in the beginning. Rather than cutting them out entirely forevermore, just put them aside for a while. You may want to revisit them (in moderation) in the future, once your new habits are stronger than sugar's influence over you.

As tempting as it might be to become a zealot once you've read about the harmful effects of sugar, try to refrain from an extreme, immediate switch. While this method might work for a few, you'll likely benefit from a softer approach of integrating healthier foods into your diet while gradually reducing the foods you now know aren't as friendly.

It is also good to be aware of the way you frame your food choices to those around you. It can be off-putting to people to constantly be told about what you or they 'should' or 'should not' be eating, doing and thinking; and it can actually have the opposite effect to the one you intend, which is to help. Your best friend and ally here is to be a healthy and gentle example.

This next part is kind of like a 'Choose your own adventure'. It's very rewarding to make changes to your health and feel hopeful again about being able to transform the way you feel, think and look. Some people take to change and newness easily and if that's you, great! Get into it – you can skip to page 20! Some people, however, have a long history of battling with themselves and being their own harshest critic. If this has been your way in the past and you're feeling a little nervous about implementing what you learn, then this section is for you. Read on!

'Be a healthy and gentle example.'

❮ REAL FOOD AURA

CHANGING YOUR THINKING

The following suggestions are based simply on commonsense and my own experience of what has worked for Damon and me.

Firstly, congratulate yourself. You're about to learn how to be kind to yourself on every level. In fact, you are already taking steps towards this by reading this guide.

Start by giving yourself the praise you would like to receive from another for being brave and trying something new. You may want to do this in the form of direct self-praise by just thinking the thought, or you may choose to stick a Post-it note on your desk. Something simple and direct will do, such as 'Go me' or, my personal choice, 'Well done'.

Now be upfront and acknowledge you're human by accepting you may stumble first before you learn to walk and then run. Promise yourself now that if or when any stumbles occur, you will handle yourself gently. Know it may be tricky at times to navigate your way among the people and situations that will test your resolve.

Rather than being harsh when you perceive yourself as having 'failed' or 'slipped up', start to change your viewpoint and language. For example, self-talk may have previously sounded like this: 'What have I done? I never stick to these things. I've gone backwards. I've failed. Oh well, I might as well give up and go back to my old ways. It's too hard, I can't do it. Time to rent *Dirty Dancing* and eat a hundred doughnuts . . .'

Instead try something more like this:

'Okay, so that decision wasn't ideal. I don't feel too good right now. Still, it reminded me why I made the choice to try things differently. I'm glad I am learning to make new choices. It's good to be learning what works for me and what no longer fits. Next time I'll know exactly how to handle that situation because I've learnt what I could do better from the way I handled it this time. Hmm, starting to feel better about it already. Yay me!'

Now, from this point on I recommend you be kind to yourself. You will do this by choosing one of the following options:

a) Pat yourself on the back.

b) Give yourself a wee hug.

c) Kiss your own lovely little paw.

If this seems trite or silly, it's because it's meant to be! Humour is an antidote to almost anything. If you're giggling, at least you won't be beating yourself up. You'll struggle to chastise yourself when you remember me telling you to 'Kiss your own lovely little paw!'

So please try it. Do it now.

Pat, hug or kiss.

Cute, huh? Makes you chuckle a little bit? Makes me chuckle.

Now, whenever you take a positive step towards doing things differently, be it cooking a recipe from this book, saying no to your old habits or practising kind self-talk, I want you to kiss or hug yourself, or pat yourself on the back. Very soon it will become internalised and you won't have to walk around doing it – unless you want to, of course (wouldn't the world be a happier place?!). Until this happens though, it's best you keep doing it. It's silly, it's fun and it works. I've done it – even when it felt naff – and it worked for me. I discovered it's actually very profound to give yourself the praise you might never get otherwise.

'Be kind to yourself.'

KITCHEN NOTES

So you've made the exciting decision to try eating differently for a while and observe the effects on your health and wellbeing. Here are some tips to help you on your way.

Using up your sugary stuff

Some families prefer using up what they've already got while gradually incorporating more healthful foods into the kitchen. Others will want to have an 'Out with the old, in with the new' approach and haul out the sugary stuff.

You might like to donate to charity those ingredients that are still in unopened tins or boxes. Alternatively, you could offer half-opened items to a neighbour or friend who has staunchly told you they never ever intend to see *That Sugar Film* or read *That Sugar Book* and couldn't care less!

The Kombucha recipe (see page 115) is the only recipe in this book which uses actual sugar – although it is totally 'eaten' by the bacteria as it ferments. You may want to hold on to your sugar for this purpose alone; it's up to you.

Above all, know thyself! If it's too risky for you to dabble in the sweet stuff, then don't tempt yourself: just clean out the cupboards and you'll avoid late-night wanderings into the kitchen with the intention of having 'just one' biscuit. If you are pretty good with moderating yourself, you can be more flexible.

Good fats

I cook with butter and coconut oil, which both have a high smoke point (they don't turn rancid with regular cooking heats, unlike other oils). I use extra virgin olive oil and avocado oil for drizzling on salads. We avoid canola oil, corn oil, sunflower oil and cottonseed oil. See page 54 for more about good fats.

Salt and pepper

I don't tend to season my meals with salt and pepper as I like the other flavours to shine through, but feel free to season to your taste. When a recipe calls for salt, I use Celtic sea salt or pink Himalayan salt as they are said to contain higher levels of trace minerals than regular table salt.

Do I need any special kitchen equipment?

I use the following bits of equipment to make cooking easy and enjoyable.

A good high-speed blender that can deal with nuts and vegetables for smoothies, sauces and soups is essential. You don't need the top of the line, just a decent-enough quality to get started.

A food processor is fantastic for turning leftovers into different meals. You could chop (but the bits will be big) and you could blend (but it would become too pureed), but a food processor delivers the ideal in-between consistency with ease. I was resistant at first (no room in the kitchen!) but now I'm converted. You can pick them up second-hand or buy a small cheap one to get you started.

Good sharp knives are a must-have. Go and get them sharpened: a blunt knife is actually more dangerous because it can slip.

A large frying pan with a glass lid is not essential, but I find it incredibly handy. The lid helps cook things evenly and the glass allows you to keep an eye on the sizzle factor without having to lift the lid and let the heat out.

A spiraliser is your new best friend. Get the kids involved and let them have some fun in the kitchen learning how to turn veggies into pasta.

Zoe

21

SHOULD I BUY ORGANIC?

The goal of these recipes is to get you eating more whole foods. The freshest ingredients will always have the most flavour so try and purchase these wherever possible. Whether or not they are organic is totally up to you.

The first argument usually presented when it comes to buying organic ingredients is the expense. I get it. We are lucky enough to live near an amazing organic co-op. The lady who runs it grows half the produce on her own sustainable farm, which cuts the transportation and delivery costs considerably. She's a single mother who is passionate about sustainability and ecology and I have watched her build her farm from scratch with gumption and sheer love for what she does. The freshness of her produce is unquestionable and the flavour is rich and deep. The low prices are astonishing.

I really respect and want to support people who are doing things differently, going against the grain and putting ethics and responsibility for the planet and people above all else. I'd rather the hardworking independent farmer pocket our dough even if it means we spend less on other things. Damon still gets a bit grumpy sometimes when I insist on buying particular organic produce, but I often remind him that we don't buy bottles of fancy wine anymore so our indulgence is good produce. This often quells the beast!

We still buy non-organic fruits and vegetables but I wash them when I can. I figure we wouldn't drink pesticide, so why eat it? Once I get the fruit and vegetables home from the supermarket, I soak them in a bucket of water with a splash of apple cider vinegar for about 10 minutes. Then I give them a good shake around, tip the water out, drain them dry and pop them in the fridge so they are ready to go when we need them.

If budget is your main focus, then buy cheap and wash well. If you can afford to do half and half, then have a look at the list opposite to see which foods are best to buy organic and which are less important.

Finally, if you have the space, time and energy to grow your own like a green-thumbed legend, then do so! That's my ultimate dream: to have a wonderful vegetable garden that we can all potter in and enjoy sharing with our family and friends.

BUY ORGANIC IF YOU CAN

apples

grapes

nectarines

peaches

strawberries

capsicum

celery

cherry tomatoes

cucumber

potato

spinach

sugar snap peas

BUY CONVENTIONAL

kiwi

mango

papaya

grapefruit

pineapple

rockmelon

asparagus

avocado

cabbage

cauliflower

eggplant

onion

peas (frozen)

sweetcorn

sweet potato

COMMONLY CALLED THE DiRTY DOZEN™ AND THE CLEAN FiFTEEN™, THiS LiST, COMPILED ANNUALLY BY THE ENViRONMENTAL WORKiNG GROUP, DENOTES THE FRUiT AND VEG WiTH THE HiGHEST AND LOWEST LEVELS OF PESTiCiDE RESiDUE. FiND OUT MORE AT EWG.ORG.

the
BRIDGING WEEK

the BRIDGING WEEK

The recipes in this section have been carefully chosen to help ease you off a high-sugar diet. Please don't think you have to eat the recipes every day – some days you may just prefer simple poached eggs or natural Greek-style yoghurt with berries. These recipes are designed to open you up to new delicious food ideas that don't involve sugar or other refined carbohydrates. Most also contain elements that are emotionally comforting or nurturing (foods you could bathe in, is what I like to call them . . . although I don't recommend a bath of cauliflower risotto balls – the cheese tends to stick to the sides).

When I talked earlier about what happens to your body when you reduce sugar (see page 6), I deliberately prioritised the mental and internal health benefits. This is because the focus with new ways of eating is often on weight loss and we end up neglecting other pivotal factors. A telling stat now reveals that a small percentage of obese people are actually metabolically healthy on the inside while 20 per cent of 'skinny' people are metabolically unhealthy (disturbingly the number shoots up for teenagers to around 40 per cent). This is why we sometimes hear the story of the seemingly fighting-fit man in his early forties who suddenly drops dead of a heart attack while out running. In some of these cases, the problems were on the inside and may not have been outwardly apparent at all. There is now evidence to support sugar being a major player, if not *the* major player, in determining metabolic health.

That said, the following recipes may well have an effect on your weight. They certainly did for me. Over the past 15 years there have been 25 randomised controlled trials (the gold standard of medical studies) showing the benefits of a lower-carbohydrate diet in regards to weight loss and metabolic health. These studies surpass results seen with calorie counting or low-fat diets (read the terrific book *Slimology: The Relatively Simple Science of Slimming* by Sam Feltham for more info). Let me explain . . .

GOODBYE REFINED CARBS *(for now)*

Because I was trying to lose weight quickly and also reduce my pre type 2 diabetes and heart-disease risks, I wanted to keep my insulin levels down. In simple terms, insulin is our 'fuel partitioning' hormone, which means it decides whether to store our fuel as fat or burn it for energy.

The catch is that if we have lots of glucose in the bloodstream (which foods like bread and pasta break down to), then insulin has to deal with it. And when insulin is dealing with all that glucose, it shuts down our fat-burning processes and we are unable to use fat for energy. So imagine us eating 30 to 40 teaspoons of sugar a day, plus toast in the morning and pasta for dinner – now that is an absolutely cranking glucose/insulin dance party in our bloodstream, which results in very few opportunities for the body to burn off fat (plus the excess glucose can also be stored as fat, but that's a whole other story).

When I was turning my health around after the experiment, I avoided all sugary foods and refined carbs and my body loved me for it. We get all the glucose we require from whole fruits and vegetables and the occasional wholegrain if we are healthy and active. Our culture is saturated with refined carbohydrates and our bodies simply haven't evolved to deal with the amount we are eating. That's not to say you can never eat these foods again but for this transitional period, I recommend avoiding them to keep that insulin down.

Zoe and I are very excited to be able to share what worked for me. If you commit to looking at food in a new and nourishing way and seeing it as the prime tool for determining how you think and feel about the world, you won't even miss these foods – and your body will thank you for years to come.

ADDED SUGARS *versus* NATURAL SUGARS

Throughout this journey, the most recurrent social-media discussion point has been around the difference between natural and added sugars. What's good for me? What's bad for me? How much is too much? And is my smoothie with two mangos, three bananas and some apple juice okay as long as it is made in an enzyme-preserving NutriBullet that I paid heaps for?

To get some answers, I think we should turn to a body known as the World Health Organization (WHO). I'm fairly sure that with a title like that, they are pretty serious about what they do, and don't make statements lightly.

Although it may have appeared planned because the timing was *so* good, the WHO released their new recommendations around sugar intake on the exact same day we opened the film in Australia. We asked them to come to our opening-night red-carpet event but they were busy – with world health. (We also asked the band The Who by mistake, but got no response.)

The WHO recommend that for optimal health we should restrict our 'free or added sugar' intake to just 25 grams or 6 teaspoons a day, based on a 2000-calories-a-day diet. Okay and thanks, but what the hell do you mean?

Well, the simple rule is this:

Sugars naturally occurring in fruits, vegetables and dairy are okay, but we need to be wary of sugars removed from their original source and added to foods. These are referred to as 'free' or added sugars, and are usually added to foods as a sweetener or as a preservative for a longer shelf-life.

So when you are out shopping, it's important to check the ingredients list on food labels and look out for these sugars (listed opposite). Often straightforward 'sugar' will be listed, but beware! Companies are getting cheeky and in a bid to avoid using the word 'sugar' on their labels, they are increasingly using other names as a disguise – my favourite is 'grape mist'. They are also employing a sneaky tactic called 'fragmentation', which means that even though sugar may be the predominant ingredient in the product, if these other cheeky names are used instead, then the word 'sugar' doesn't need to appear at the top of the list – the load is carried by the others.

What you need to know is that all of these inventive names 'carrying the load' are still the 'free or added sugars' the World Health dudes talk about and many of them contain fructose as a sweetener.

TAKE THE GENTLE APPROACH
EXPERTS i HAVE SPOKEN TO SUGGEST THAT
ANYTHiNG UNDER 5 GRAMS OF SUGAR PER
100 GRAMS iN A PRODUCT iS OKAY TO KEEP
iN THE PANTRY. YOU MiGHT EVENTUALLY CUT
BACK ON THESE FOODS, BUT AS A START,
TREAT YOURSELF AND YOUR FAMiLY WiTH
KINDNESS AND TAKE THE GENTLE APPROACH.

The WHO

6 Teaspoons a Day

60 DIFFERENT NAMES FOR SUGAR

Agave

Barbados sugar

Barley malt

Beet sugar

Beet concentrate

Blackstrap molasses

Brown rice syrup
(no fructose but still considered an 'added sugar' by WHO)

Buttered sugar

Buttered syrup

Cane juice crystals

Cane juice

Cane sugar

Caramel

Carob syrup

Caster sugar

Coconut sugar

Corn sweetener

Corn syrup

Corn syrup solids

Crystal line fructose

Date sugar

Demara sugar

Dextran

Dextrose

Diastatic malt

Diatase

Ethyl maltol

Evaporated cane juice

Fructose

Fruit juice concentrate

Golden sugar

Golden syrup

Grape sugar

Grape concentrate

Grape mist

High fructose corn syrup

Honey

Invert sugar

Icing sugar

Malt syrup

Maltodextrin

Maltose

Maple syrup

Molasses syrup

Muscovado

Organic raw sugar

Oat syrup

Panela

Panocha

Confectioner's sugar

Rice bran syrup

Rice syrup

Sorghum

Sorghum syrup

Sucrose

Syrup

Treacle

Tapioca syrup

Turbinado

Yellow sugar

CAN I STILL EAT FRUIT?

Just to recap, fructose is what makes foods taste sweet. It is found in fruit (and small amounts in vegetables), but there is a big difference between consuming it as fruit and consuming it as a 'free' sugar. Fructose in fruit is encased in fibre, which significantly affects its metabolism in our bodies. The fibre helps to slow down the absorption so the sugar doesn't get fast, direct access to the liver like it does when it is 'free'. (The best theory I have heard for fructose being sweet is so animals would be attracted to fruit, eat it and release the seed from within.) This is why I often have to shout very loudly or write frequently on social media that we absolutely endorse eating fruit.

However, it's good to know that we are all different when it comes to how much fruit we can eat. The current recommendation in Australia is about 2 serves a day – but this is based on the assumption that you aren't having 30 teaspoons of 'free' sugars in other products. Those with type 2 diabetes are advised to reduce their fruit intake while others, like an Australian cricketer or the incredibly aggressive man who occasionally baits me on social media, can be perfectly fine on 10 bananas a day. It all depends on a range of factors such as hormones, genetics, exercise regimes, metabolic health and even gut bacteria. If you are concerned, it's worth talking to a nutritionist about how much fruit is right for your needs.

And as for the NutriBullet fruit smoothie, well, many experts on my travels told me that making a smoothie is fine as long as you stick to roughly the same amount of fruit you could eat on its own with the fibre intact. So if that's only half an apple, a few strawberries and a banana, then try to make sure that's all that goes into the turbo-charged, mega-blending, fruit-obliteration device. I would suggest not indulging in too many salubrious smoothie sessions while transitioning from a high-sugar diet though. Your body may be able to handle it one day, but not quite yet. Remember that lovely bath you were giving your liver earlier? Well, no one likes having sticky pureed fruit dumped on them when they're trying to relax in the tub.

So, in summary, the sugar in fruit is fine when it's in whole form or occasionally pulverised, but as the World Health heavyweights now stipulate, once that sugar is 'removed' from its natural casing, it has a very different effect on our bodies. This 'free' sugar (such as that found in fruit juices and syrups) should be kept to 6 teaspoons or under for optimal health.

'We are all different when it comes to how much fruit we can eat.'

DRIED FRUIT

Dried fruit often contains a very high level of concentrated sugar. A piece of dried fruit on its own isn't a major problem: it's the quantity we're able to consume, compared with eating fruit in its whole form.

I did an experiment for the film (although it didn't make the cut) that explained this very clearly. I counted out a box of sultanas and discovered there are around 90 in a box. I then tried to eat 90 grapes (what a sultana is before it's dried). I reached about 25 before the fibre and water in the whole fruit told my body that I was full; it didn't allow me to access all that sugar. However, once we remove the water from the fruit, its structure changes and we can consume a huge hit of concentrated sugar without feeling full. And as we are now discovering, we simply haven't evolved to deal with that sugar load. So while there's no doubt eating dried fruit will deliver more nutritional benefits than smashing a Mars Bar, it's worth making sure you don't overload on those that have clearly spent too long on a beach in Bali.

UNDERSTANDING LACTOSE

The other important point to understand involves lactose, a natural sugar found in dairy products. (Stephen Fry explains this with a rhyming couplet in the film and the previous book.) If you are reading a label for plain unsweetened milk, you will notice it still has a fair bit of sugar in it. This is lactose; it is not a 'free' or added sugar. Flavoured milks, however, are different – they contain natural lactose, *plus* added sugar for sweetness. This also applies to yoghurt. The naturally occurring lactose in yoghurt equates to just over 1 teaspoon per 100 grams (4.7 grams), so any more than that is going to be added sugar. Always check the ingredients list on flavoured yoghurt and look for those cheeky sugar names mentioned on page 31 just to be sure.

This label below is a great example. According to the label, this yoghurt contains 20 grams of sugar per serving size of 170 grams. First, we check the ingredients and what do we see? 'Evaporated cane juice' plus 'fruit concentrate': both are cheeky names for sugar. Busted.

And now we'll do the maths for you to show you exactly how much added sugar is in this yoghurt. A teaspoon of sugar is 4 grams; so 20 grams divided by four equals 5 teaspoons of sugar. As we now know, when it comes to dairy products, 1 teaspoon per 100 grams is lactose. This means that in a 170-gram serving size there are 1.7 teaspoons of natural sugar. So 5 teaspoons in total minus the 1.7 teaspoons of lactose leaves 3.3. There we have it. There are over 3 teaspoons of added or 'free' sugars in this yoghurt. That's half your daily recommended WHO amount in one serve. You can start to see how easily the sugar can add up in your day.

Nutrition Facts

Serving Size: 170g
Servings Per Container 1

Calories 140
    Calories from Fat 0

*Percent Daily Values (DV) are based on a 2,000 calorie diet.

Amount Per Serving	% Daily Value	Amount Per Serving	%Daily Value
Total Fat 0g	0%	**Total Carbohydrate** 20g	7%
Saturated Fat 0g	0%	Dietary Fiber less than 1g	4%
Trans Fat 0g		Sugars 20g	
Cholesterol 0mg	0%	**Protein** 14g	28%
Sodium 65mg	3%		
Vitamin A 0% • Vitamin C 2% • Calcium 20% • Iron 0%			

KEEP REFRIGERATED

INGREDIENTS: NONFAT YOGHURT (CULTURED PASTEURIZED NONFAT MILK, LIVE AND ACTIVE CULTURES: S. THERMOPHILUS, L. BULGARICUS, L. ACIDOPHILUS, BIFIOUS AND L. CASEI). FRUIT ON THE BOTTOM (STRAWBERRIES, EVAPORATED CANE JUICE, PECTIN, NATURAL FLAVOURS, LOCUST BEAN GUM, FRUIT AND VEGETABLE JUICE CONCENTRATE [FOR COLOUR]).

FLAVOURED YOGHURT

Good thing we have some delicious ideas for flavoured yoghurt without all that added sugar. Use full-fat organic natural (no added sugar) Greek-style yoghurt and simply add one of the following combinations, depending on what you like and what's in season.

These ingredients can be blended to make your own flavoured yoghurt.

sliced banana, fresh figs and passionfruit

blueberries and peach wedges

coconut flakes and cacao nibs

a mixture of berries: raspberries, strawberries and blackberries

cherries and nectarine wedges

A NEW TEASPOON LABELLING SYSTEM

It has become very obvious that we need much clearer labelling on food products when it comes to sugar. So here is a proposal.

It is very simple and is based on the new World Health Organization recommendations of no more than 6 teaspoons a day of added or 'free' sugars for optimal health (explained on page 30). People need to be able to clearly calculate how much sugar they are having in a day.

There are basically two symbols we are proposing: one for the total number of teaspoons of sugar in a product and one for the natural sugar and added sugars that are present in dairy products.

If any sugar was added to a product by the manufacturer, we would refer to this statement from WHO:

'Free sugars refer to monosaccharides (such as glucose, fructose) and disaccharides (such as sucrose or table sugar) added to foods and drinks by the manufacturer, cook or consumer, and sugars naturally present in honey, syrups, fruit juices and fruit juice concentrates.'

Meaning, if any of the above sugars were added, the consumer would see this logo clearly on the bottle:

In general, anytime the 'total sugars' symbol was seen, this would refer to added sugars. The only exception would be dairy products, which have a combination of naturally occurring lactose sugar and added sugars. The WHO statement on natural sugars is:

'The WHO guideline (on sugar intake) does not refer to the sugars in fresh fruits and vegetables, and sugars naturally present in milk, because there is no reported evidence of adverse effects of consuming these sugars.'

This means there would be no teaspoon symbol for fresh fruits or vegetables. However, on dairy products, like flavoured yoghurt, there would be this logo, which shows the natural and added sugars present with a plus sign in the middle so you also know the total sugar content:

The team and I have been actively pushing to have this symbol placed on products and have already had some terrific expressions of interest. We will be encouraging more companies to jump on board. Check out thatsugarfilm.com for more information. Please let us know what you think.

VERY FEW PEOPLE CAN ACTUALLY PULL OFF DOUBLE DENIM (EXCEPT FOR ZOE & VELVET).

ARTIFICIAL SWEETENERS

'Once you move away from refined sugars, artificial sweeteners will start to taste unpleasant.'

In the teased hair and spandex days of the mid-1980s, counting calories was as popular as a Bon Jovi album. In this climate, diet soft drinks were an effervescent masterstroke from the soda giants. 'Just One Calorie!' proclaimed the greased-lensed commercials showing 'double-denimed' twenty-somethings with jeans to the navel, skipping along beaches, laughing at each other's faux abandon. They were carefree, pimple-free and sugar-free, and diet soda was the reason why.

The power of this marketing still pervades our culture today. But ladies and gentlemen, I am here to inform you that not only is counting calories a ludicrously simplistic view of staying healthy but, perhaps more profoundly, very few people can actually pull off double denim.

Let's strip back the faded acid wash, turn to trusty science and learn some truths about our artificial family of unfortunate names. Let's meet little aspartame, sucralose, neotame, saccharin, stevia and poor old Acesulfame K (or Ace to his friends).

First up, a disclaimer: artificial sweeteners do have their place. For some people, they can be handy during a transition phase; almost like methadone for sugar addicts. However, the nutritionists and dieticians I met on my travels recommended artificial sweeteners *only* for those transitioning from an incredibly high-sugar diet. And only just.

The current darling of the sugar pretenders is a natural sweetener called stevia, which is what I think you would call your child if you loved the name Steve but had a daughter. You can buy it in a highly processed form from the supermarket or you can purchase a plant from Bunnings and simply pull off a leaf and throw it into your tea. But before we get reductionist and check what the lab says, there's a very simple message here: we need to move away from the idea that things need to taste sweet to be good.

When I lowered my sugar consumption post-experiment, I was shocked at how quickly I experienced 'paladjustment' (see page 14), to the point where a banana is now sweet to me. When you reach that point, you don't crave the sweet hit anymore – and you certainly don't crave or need a *fake* sweet hit. I promise that once you move away from refined sugars and move to natural, real foods, artificial sweeteners will start to taste unpleasant. You will detect the metallic, industrial processing that gave birth to them and will want to wash your mouth out with something from the Mother Nature catalogue.

But if you think I am just on some hocus-pocus hippy rant, then here's some important and very earnest science to get you over the line:

A 14-year study of 66,118 women, published in the American Journal of Clinical Nutrition, discovered that women who drank diet soft drinks drank twice as much as those who drank regular sugar-sweetened soft drinks. This is because artificial sweeteners can be addictive and are much sweeter than regular sugar; I explain the sweetness factor over the page. Women who drank one can of diet soft drink a day had a 33 per cent increased risk of type 2 diabetes. (This result needs to be treated with caution, as there are many other factors at play. The authors of the study take the time to outline these additional factors and they are alluded to in the next point.)

Other studies have shown that the sugar pretenders can trick the body into thinking that food is on the way. They kick-start your metabolism, which means you start pumping out insulin, that frustratingly efficient hormone that likes to store fat in our bodies (see page 28).

Artificial sweeteners can also affect our appetite-control centre. Because the body doesn't get the full caloric hit from the pretender, it feels ripped off and will search out its reward somewhere else, which means you may end up nailing a pizza with BBQ sauce or a caramel-glazed Krispy Kreme doughnut.

Studies on rats have also shown that when artificial sweeteners are mixed with real sugar, the rats consume more, so the 'super combo' drives even more consumption. (This is particularly interesting given Coke's latest offering, 'Coke Life', is stevia mixed with 10 teaspoons of sugar in a 600 ml bottle.)

SCIENTISTS AT THE THE WEIZMANN INSTITUTE OF SCIENCE IN ISRAEL HAVE ALSO CONDUCTED SOME INTERESTING STUDIES ON ARTIFICIAL SWEETENERS AND THE MICROBIOME OR GUT BACTERIA. THEIR HUMAN TRIALS SUGGEST THAT IN MANY PEOPLE THE SWEETENERS CAN ALSO CREATE GLUCOSE INTOLERANCE WHICH COULD BE CONTRIBUTING TO OBESITY AND TYPE 2 DIABETES.

HERE'S SOME MORE CHARACTER PROFILING OF 'THE PRETENDERS' →

ASPARTAME

More cuddly name: Equal and NutraSweet

Lurks: in diet soft drinks (Diet Coke, Coke Zero) and sugar-free gum

What you should know: It is 200 times sweeter than sugar. It is made from Aspartic acid, which doesn't sound like something you'd want in your body. And the kicker: aspartame accounts for over 75 per cent of the adverse reactions to food additives reported to the FDA (according to Mark D. Gold from the Aspartame Toxicity Information Center). Many of these reactions are very serious, including seizures.

SUCRALOSE

More positive, 'derivative-of-something-joyous' name: Splenda

Lurks: in soft drinks, frozen desserts, cereals and baked goods

What you should know: It is roughly 600 times sweeter than sugar. It was actually developed by the sugar company Tate & Lyle. The Center for Science in the Public Interest downgraded sucralose from 'safe' to 'caution' in June 2013. Anything downgraded from 'safe' isn't entering my system.

NEOTAME

Less 'sounding-like-a-substance-you'd-find-on-another-planet' name: NutraSweet (improved formula)

Lurks: not on the market yet

What you should know: The new kid on the block. 8000 times sweeter than sugar. Yes, 8000. Mega sweetener. No independent studies have yet been done on it. Some speculate it may be worse than aspartame. I would rather eat real sugar.

SACCHARIN

More 'kind-and-unobtrusive' name: Sweet'N Low

Lurks: Appeared in the cult classic diet soda, Tab. Also frequents toothpaste and some medicines.

What you should know: Around since 1879, it is 300 times sweeter than sugar and is known for its 'delicious' metallic aftertaste. Saccharin has been linked to bladder cancer in rats, and even though no conclusive evidence has emerged around cancer in humans, I would be using it sparingly.

ACESULFAME K

The 'any-name-is-better-than-that name' name: Sunett, Sweet One, and Sweet & Safe (see what they did there?)

Lurks: Very popular and pops up in baked goods, beverages (Coke Zero), pharmaceutical and oral hygiene products, plus confectionary and chewing gum

What you should know: 200 times sweeter than sugar. It is often blended with other artificial sweeteners and is used in around 4000 foods and drinks. It will be listed in the ingredient statement of a packaged food or beverage as 'Acesulfame potassium'. Or 'No thanks, I'll have water' in English.

STEVIA

The 'tell-it-as-it-is name' or 'more-nature-sounding' name: Stevia, Natvia.

Lurks: Coke Life, many sugar-free recipes, yoghurts, other food items

What you should know: Comes from a plant in Paraguay (and can now be bought at Bunnings). Often highly refined and sold at supermarkets. It is 300 times sweeter than sugar. While the US FDA does generally recognise this sweetener as safe, Jennifer Nelson, director of clinical dietetics at the Mayo Clinic in Minnesota, recommends using stevia in moderation. It is seen as a natural sweetener as opposed to an artificial one and reports suggest it doesn't affect blood-sugar levels in the same way that other pretenders do. Handy as a transition off a high-sugar diet but use sparingly so the palate can adjust and you can move away from things needing to be sweet to be good.

What much of this pretender profiling points to – and the studies are beginning to back this up – is that these artificial sweeteners, and especially those found in brilliantly marketed 'weight loss' aluminium cans, can actually contribute to weight gain and poor metabolic health. Whether it's the actual drink itself or the fact that they encourage you to consume more is still not entirely clear and more studies are needed.

The bottom line is to avoid the fake stuff altogether if you can and just have an occasional real treat and thoroughly enjoy it! You'd actually be better off with that approach instead of constantly turning to a pretender who really isn't doing you any good, who skips with an insincere laugh on the beach and, let's face it, whose stonewash pleated denim jeans are pulled up way too high.

ARE YOU DRINKING ENOUGH WATER?

7 GLASSES

6 GLASSES

5 GLASSES

4 GLASSES

3 GLASSES

2 GLASSES

1 GLASS

HERE ARE SOME TIPS TO GET YOU DRINKING MORE:

Take your own water bottle with you in the car, on the bus and to work.

Personalise the bottle. This gives a sense of 'ownership', so you won't leave it behind somewhere. Make it fun for children: stickers or drawings are good.

If you are new to the water-drinking caper, buy a reusable plastic or aluminium bottle and mark the number of glasses up the side in permanent marker. This way you can see how many glasses you are drinking per day, and this will make you feel good.

Consciously change your habits: get into the routine of drinking a glass of water when you wake up, and ordering water with every meal.

Set a reminder on your phone or computer to drink three times a day. There are apps that send reminders now, and the new Apple Watch can even send an electric jolt to your wrist. Nothing like an electrocution to get you drinking water.

Put up a chart on the kitchen wall for the kids. Set a challenge – 20 glasses of water a week as a start. Do they get a reward if they reach the goal?

Take an empty soda or juice bottle and every time you would normally buy a sugary drink, put a 2-dollar coin in it and drink water instead. You will be getting healthy *and* saving money.

Some of you may find water a bit dull early on while the 'paladjustment' occurs, so over the page you'll find some creative ideas from Zoe to bring a thumping dance party to your H_2O. . .

ZOE

FLAVOURED WATER

SPARKLING WATER

½ cup whole or gently
crushed raspberries

½ cup whole or gently
crushed blackberries

2 cups mint leaves
(you can leave them on the stem)

⅓ cup passionfruit seeds
and juice

STILL WATER

good ole lemon or lime slices

1 Lebanese cucumber,
thinly sliced lengthways

½ cup pomegranate seeds
(these will also turn the water
a delicate pink)

1 cup frozen mandarin segments

½ cup frozen green grapes

Firstly, again be kind to yourself. You are not 'quitting' your favourite sugary beverage; you are discovering new and interesting ways to enjoy different options! Make this a fun exercise for yourself and your family and get creative with your own natural herb, vegetable and fruit flavourings.

If you're used to fizzy soft drinks, your new best friend will be natural sparkling water. This will give you the 'mouth feel' (this is my favourite term I learnt from Damon during the experiment) and the sensation of fizz without the junk.

To jazz things up while your palate is still adjusting, try adding one of the flavour suggestions (top left) to a litre of sparkling water.

Once you've adjusted, or if you prefer, you can get creative with still water. See left for simple flavouring ideas.

HERBAL TEAS

In winter we drink plenty of herbal tea. Some of our favourite brews include chai, jasmine, lavender, chamomile, mint and rooibos. There are so many wonderful tea shops around nowadays with blends from all over the world. Some herbs impart a sense of sweetness despite having no added sugar in them: keep an eye out for teas containing cinnamon, licorice and fennel. For a refreshing summer brew, allow the tea to cool, then refrigerate it or add ice to serve.

. . . .

Some more tips! For a relaxing bedtime beverage, tie five lavender stems together with some rinsed twine and add to a bottle of water. Or visit your grandma and while you're there, nip into her garden and snip a few violets, nasturtiums or any other edible flowers. Freeze them with some water in an ice-cube tray. Serve with either still or sparkling water – the flowers will have little or no flavour, but they are so darn pretty you'll forgive them and maybe even forget you are drinking plain old H_2O!

I also recommended kombucha (see page 115). It has a really satisfying bubbly fizz and a dense aromatic flavour – why not give it a try?

CACAO HOT CHOCCY *or* DANDELION LATTE

SERVES 2

2 cups milk
(or your milk substitute)

2 tablespoons raw cacao powder
or 1 tablespoon dandelion roots

1 teaspoon vanilla extract

1 teaspoon ground cinnamon

½ banana

Here are a couple of ideas to give you some extra nurturing and warming in the colder months. Cacao is different from cocoa. It's processed differently and retains many more restorative properties, including high levels of magnesium, which helps you sleep. Cacao is an excellent bedtime beverage.

Dandelion roots, Damon's favourite, are often used as a coffee substitute and have the same earthy richness with a nutty flavour. Dandelion can be found in the health food section of most supermarkets, although I imagine it will become more popular and readily available as people catch on to its awesomeness.

. . . .

Whizz all the ingredients together in a blender, then pop them in a small saucepan over a medium heat. When the mixture starts to bubble, remove from the heat and serve in your favourite mug.

ZOE

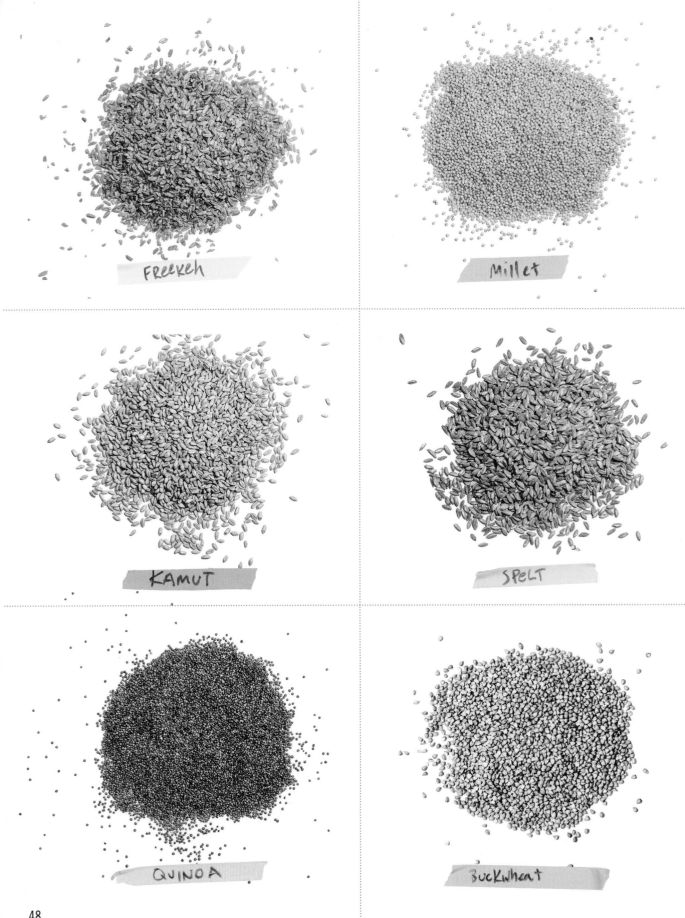

Freekeh

Millet

KAMUT

SPELT

QUINOA

Buckwheat

the GRAINS DEBATE

'When we munch on a grain is there anything to gain? Are they causing us pain and affecting our brain? People think you're insane if you don't eat grain but before you profane and jump on that train, let's take a stroll down a lane and talk facts nice and plain.' If Dr Seuss had been a nutritionist, that's how I believe he would have started this chapter.

Whenever someone asked for my opinion on grains during the Q&A sessions following the film, I always shared one story that I think sums it up and gives terrific perspective.

Luise Light should be a household name. At any trivia night, in any pub across the world, her name should be worth only 1 or 2 points. Instead, it's probably worth 10 points, or more likely it doesn't even make the questions page. This is because her name was extinguished by the might of the food industry in the early 1980s.

At the time, Luise was asked by the USDA (United States Department of Agriculture) to lead a group of top nutritionists in developing the first official 'food pyramid'. It would be a clear and comprehensive guide to assist the American public in their nutritional choices. Luise and her team committed themselves to this pyramid assembly with the same vigour that the Egyptian slaves had done centuries before (or aliens, depending on your view). They trawled through studies, engaged with biochemists and mapped out various population trends.

When the team came up for air, they had submitted a pyramid that the owners of the Luxor hotel in Las Vegas would be proud of. The bottom level, indicating foods that should be eaten the most, was a Tutankhamun tomb full of fresh fruits and vegetables. Proteins, such as eggs, nuts, fish, beans and meat (lamb 'Cheops'?), came strongly recommended, as did the liberal use of healthy fats (like 4 daily tablespoons of olive oil). Sugar was kept to a minimum and lived in the apex of the pyramid, junk foods were ruled out entirely and then there were the grains . . .

Luise and her team recommended a maximum of 2-3 serves of grains daily; 3 serves only if you were a highly active person. She explained this as no more than one sandwich a day for women and less active men. These grains were always to be eaten in whole form. Refined grains, such as the white bread, pasta and pastries that now dominate our cafes, appeared in the pyramid's apex alongside sugar. These two items were to be eaten with similar regularity – very rarely.

'Luise and her team recommended no more than one sandwich a day for women.'

Luise and her team were very proud of their work but now that the great pyramid was devised, they had to present it for review to King Khufu, who in this instance was the USDA. And because they were the Department of Agriculture, the next move was to share the pyramid with the industry they represented to get some feedback. When they handed out the culinary stone edifice for review, unsurprisingly the majority of the industries kicked up a fuss. They argued for their position and rank on the pyramid, complained about the proportions recommended to the public, and even quibbled over the particular colour of their food group. (I'm sure they also complained about there being no windows.)

What Luise and her team had presented was a smooth and functioning pyramid, perfectly aligned with nature and fit for a prosperous culture; what they got back resembled an Escher sculpture designed by a teenager on acid.

The healthy fats were removed, fruits and vegetable servings were reduced and sugar consumption was accompanied by the ambiguous phrase of 'moderate amounts'. The real Giza, however, was that the grains had ballooned from 2–3 serves of whole grains a day to an epidemic-inducing 6–11 serves, with refined grains brought down from their 'rarely eaten' penthouse apartment to the bottom level, which would sadly become the staple of the dietary guidelines and the opening act of the prestigious World Glucose Festival (Glucosetonbury?).

Luise and her team were horrified and predicted this pyramid would turn America's health into a train wreck. 'No-one needs that much bread and cereal in a day,' she said, adding that the increased servings of wheat and other grains were only to make the wheat growers happy. If approved and released to the public, Luise believed the pyramid would cause an 'unprecedented epidemic of obesity and diabetes (type 2)'. Um?

You would hope that in a decision so pivotal to the health of the human race and one that would influence generations to come that money might take a back seat temporarily. However, as we see all too frequently, financial gain (or in this case, financial grain) was firmly placed in front and the capitalist machine had to expand or die. As Denise Minger says in her terrific book, *Death By Food Pyramid*, 'Asking the Department of Agriculture to promote healthy eating was like asking Jack Daniels to promote responsible drinking; the advice could only come packaged with a wink, a nudge and a complimentary shot glass.'

In my view, through no fault of our own, we have been eating far too many grains and refined carbohydrates. Although recent 'food pyramids' and dietary guidelines have changed somewhat (Nutrition Australia now has fruits and vegetables on the bottom row), there is still literally an 'ingrained' belief that these foods are okay for us in large amounts.

'The grains had ballooned from 2–3 serves of whole grains a day to 6–11 serves.'

IT'S A BREAD BATH.

THERE IS SUBSTANTIAL EVIDENCE FOR THIS, INCLUDING FROM THE AMERICAN DIABETES ASSOCIATION AND A GREAT STUDY ENTITLED 'DIETARY CARBOHYDRATE RESTRICTION AS THE FIRST APPROACH IN DIABETES MANAGEMENT: CRITICAL REVIEW AND EVIDENCE BASE' BY RICHARD D. FEINMAN, PHD.

You only have to visit your local cafe to witness the 'bread bath' we have been soaking in: wraps, sandwiches, baguettes, croissants, bagels, pastries, muffins, pies. These have all become rock-solid staples in our diet and our bodies aren't able to deal with the amount we are consuming.

As we learnt earlier, these products interfere with our insulin levels because they break down to glucose. We cannot burn off fat when our chief 'fuel partitioning' hormone, insulin, is dealing with so much glucose. This not only affects our weight, but can wreak havoc on our metabolic pathways. Type 2 diabetes now kills someone worldwide every 6 seconds, yet was considered relatively rare before 1970. It is complete madness that some doctors and organisations still recommend solid amounts of grains to type 2 diabetics when they are fuelling the very condition the person is afflicted with.

That's why I recommend removing a lot of the refined carbohydrates in your diet, especially if you are looking to lose weight or improve metabolic conditions like type 2 diabetes or heart disease.

Shove those refined carbs firmly back where they belong and where Luise and her team intended them to be: in the apex of the pyramid (although I have referred to it as a penthouse and made it sound quite luxurious, it's actually a dusty old attic that can promote allergies).

Once you feel you're at a happy and healthy level again, or if you're a healthy person reading this, then the odd whole grain won't hurt (unless you are gluten intolerant of course, although some whole grains are gluten free). I personally don't eat too many, but Zoe enjoys them and her body deals with them perfectly well. She only cooks with ancient grains, like spelt or quinoa (which is technically a seed – that's why it's gluten free) or the brilliantly named freekeh.

'So before you refrain from eating a grain, is it the amount you eat that causes the strain? Some will choose none, like me and my brain, but I respect other's choices and won't show them disdain.' – Not Dr Seuss

GOOD FATS

Butter and coconut oil contain what is known as 'saturated fat'. For nearly 40 years, we have been told to avoid this substance as it is likely to be a major player in the role of heart disease. There have been some ugly scientific cockfighting matches in underground labs over this stuff, but recently some very big news emerged. It seems that, finally, we got some saturated *facts*.

In 2015, a report regarding the new US Dietary Guidelines appeared and then the Academy of Nutrition and Dietetics (which represents 90,000 dieticians in the US) endorsed a specific recommendation:

'We support its decision to drop dietary cholesterol from the nutrients of concern list and recommend that it similarly drop saturated fat from nutrients of concern, given lack of evidence connecting it with cardiovascular disease.'

This is a very big statement in the medical and nutrition communities and will result in some significant payouts in the cockfighting ring. Take particular notice of the words 'lack of evidence'.

Credit Suisse also recently released a comprehensive report about the future of fat. They looked at 400 studies and books on the subject. Among their key conclusions:

'Forty per cent of nutritionists and 70 per cent of General Practitioners surveyed believe that eating cholesterol-rich foods has damaging cardiovascular effects. This is not true, according to the extensive research that has become available in recent years.'

'Carbohydrates will decline from 60 per cent of global energy intake in 2011 to 55 per cent by 2030. The rising awareness of the link between excess carbohydrate consumption and metabolic syndrome, type 2 diabetes, and cardiovascular issues will largely contribute to this decrease.'

When making *That Sugar Film*, I spent a lot of time with the wonderful Professor Ken Sikaris (Professor Blood). He is a very highly regarded clinical pathologist, which means he spends his days getting to know people better than they know themselves by studying their blood through a microscope (it's pretty much stalking, if you ask me and he should be arrested).

He says that he doesn't really look as closely at cholesterol anymore when checking for heart-disease markers (science-speak for 'signs' or 'indications'). When considering heart-disease risks, a key component to look out for is triglycerides. These can come from sugar turning to fat

in the liver and then hitting the bloodstream. These little sugar-fats can interact and even oxidise with cholesterol and form the small dense and dangerous type that embeds in your artery walls. This shouldn't happen if you are keeping your added sugar consumption low.

See, we actually need cholesterol – it's very good for us (breast milk is full of it, which should tell you something) – but it's only when it mutates (by hanging out with the triglyceride gangs) that the heart needs to be wary. People tend to think there is only 'good' and 'bad' cholesterol, but it turns out there are actually two kinds of 'bad' cholesterol. And one isn't as bad as first thought.

We have long blamed cholesterol and saturated fat for heart disease, but more and more intelligent folk in white lab coats are pointing to excess refined carbohydrate consumption as being the major problem. Lower your sugar and other refined carb intake and start cooking with butter and coconut oil for a healthy, happy heart. These are old 'real foods' that have been used for centuries without alarming levels of heart disease. It's only when our dear friend Mr Sugar started to drop by more regularly that the health problems increased. I lowered my sugar intake and upped the healthy fat after the experiment and all my health 'markers' turned around in a very short space of time.

the
BRIDGING
WEEK
RECIPES

BOILED EGGS *with* BROCCOLINI *and* HALOUMI SOLDIERS

SERVES 4

4 free-range eggs

butter, for frying

200 g haloumi,
cut into long strips

2 bunches broccolini, trimmed

Here's a lesson in how to make the perfect soft-boiled egg. My golden rule? Always use a timer. (If you don't have an old-fashioned egg timer, check your phone for one.)

If you're feeling meaty, you can also add strips of crispy bacon to this recipe. Cook the bacon first, then you can fry the haloumi and broccolini in its fat rather than using butter.

And one last tip: if you don't have egg cups (or you want to mix things up a bit), you can always cut up the egg carton or use those shot glasses squirreled away in the back of the cupboard.

. . . .

Bring a saucepan of water to the boil. Once the water is bubbling, turn the heat down slightly to a rapid simmer. Set a timer for 6 minutes. Add the eggs and give them a stir.

Meanwhile, melt some butter in a large frying pan over high heat. Add the haloumi and fry quickly, flipping once so both sides brown; this should only take a minute. Remove the haloumi from the pan and place on a plate lined with paper towel.

Turn down the heat to medium and add the broccolini. Fry until the ends are a little crispy or the eggs are done – whichever comes first

Serve the soft-boiled eggs with the haloumi and broccolini on the side for dipping into the runny yolk.

VEGETARIAN   TODDLER FRIENDLY

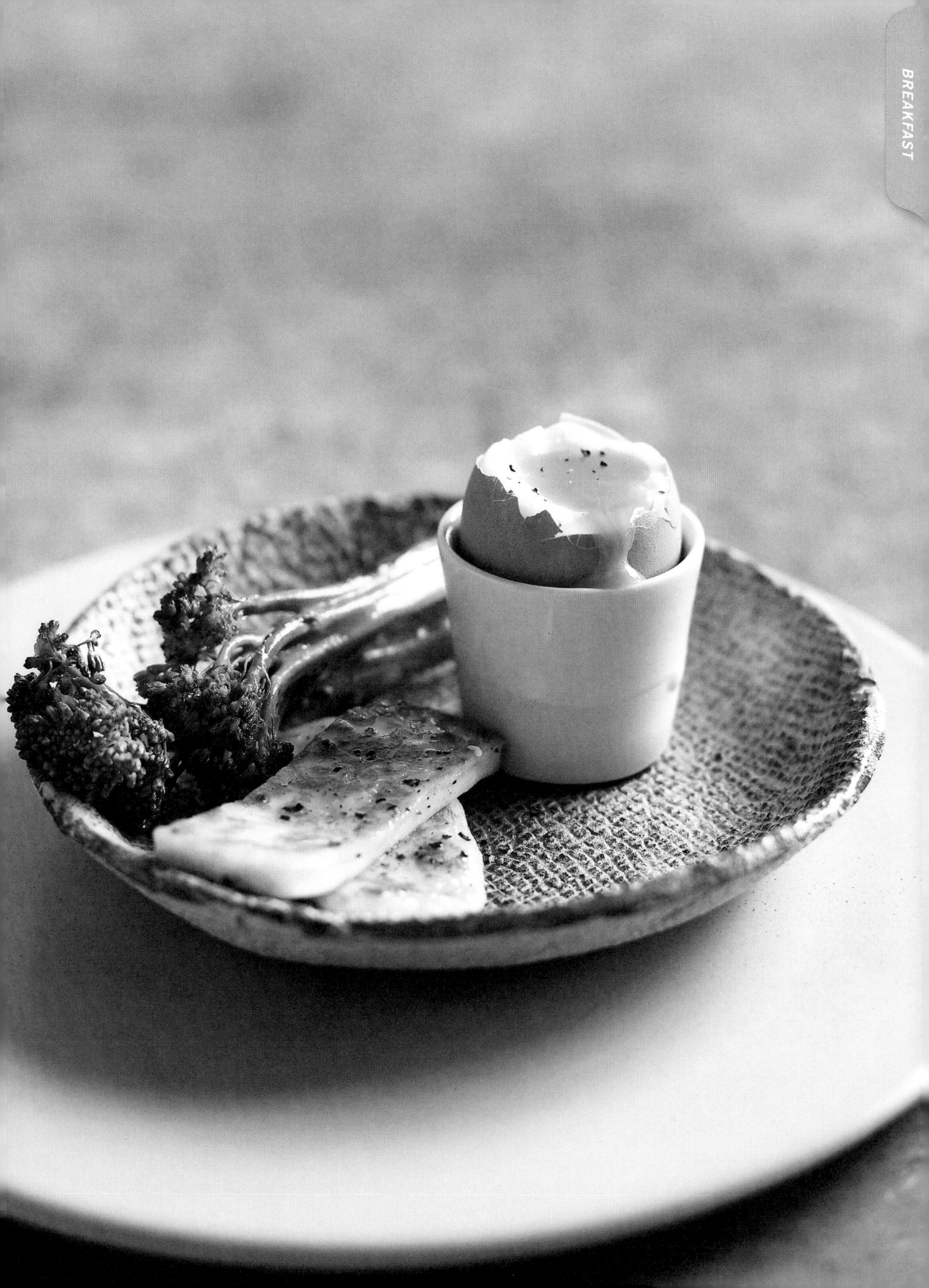

SWEET BAKED BEANS

SERVES 2

butter, for frying

1 large red onion, sliced

4 large, ripe and flavourful tomatoes

1 × 400 g tin lima beans (butter beans), drained and rinsed

baby spinach, to serve (optional)

herb sprigs, to garnish (optional)

On our travels to promote *That Sugar Film*, I met an Italian cafe owner who taught me this slow-and-low bean-cooking method. It was easily the best breakfast we sampled over three continents! Damon thought it must have contained sugar as it was so lovely and sweet, but it was just the natural sweetness of good, fresh ingredients brought out by the clever technique. The key is to keep the heat low and increase the cooking time, not the heat, if you need to. It's a good idea to make a double batch and freeze half to thaw quickly on a cold or busy morning.

Melt some butter in a large saucepan over low heat; it is essential the heat is low as this will bring out the sweet flavours. Add the onion and let it gently caramelise, stirring occasionally. Once the onion is melty and sweet, about 10–15 minutes, add the whole tomatoes. Leave them to warm for a few minutes, then crush them with the back of a wooden spoon. Stir the tomato through the caramelised onion and continue crushing them to release the juices and break up the skin.

Cover and leave to simmer very gently for about 15 minutes until rich and aromatic; add a tablespoon or two of water if necessary to keep the contents moist.

Tip in the beans and gently stir through. Pop the lid back on and leave the beans to simmer in the sauce for 30 minutes or until they are soft and starting to break apart.

Serve the beans simply on their own or with some spinach to soak up the flavours of the sauce. Garnish with herbs if you like.

VEGETARIAN   LEFTOVERS   TODDLER FRIENDLY

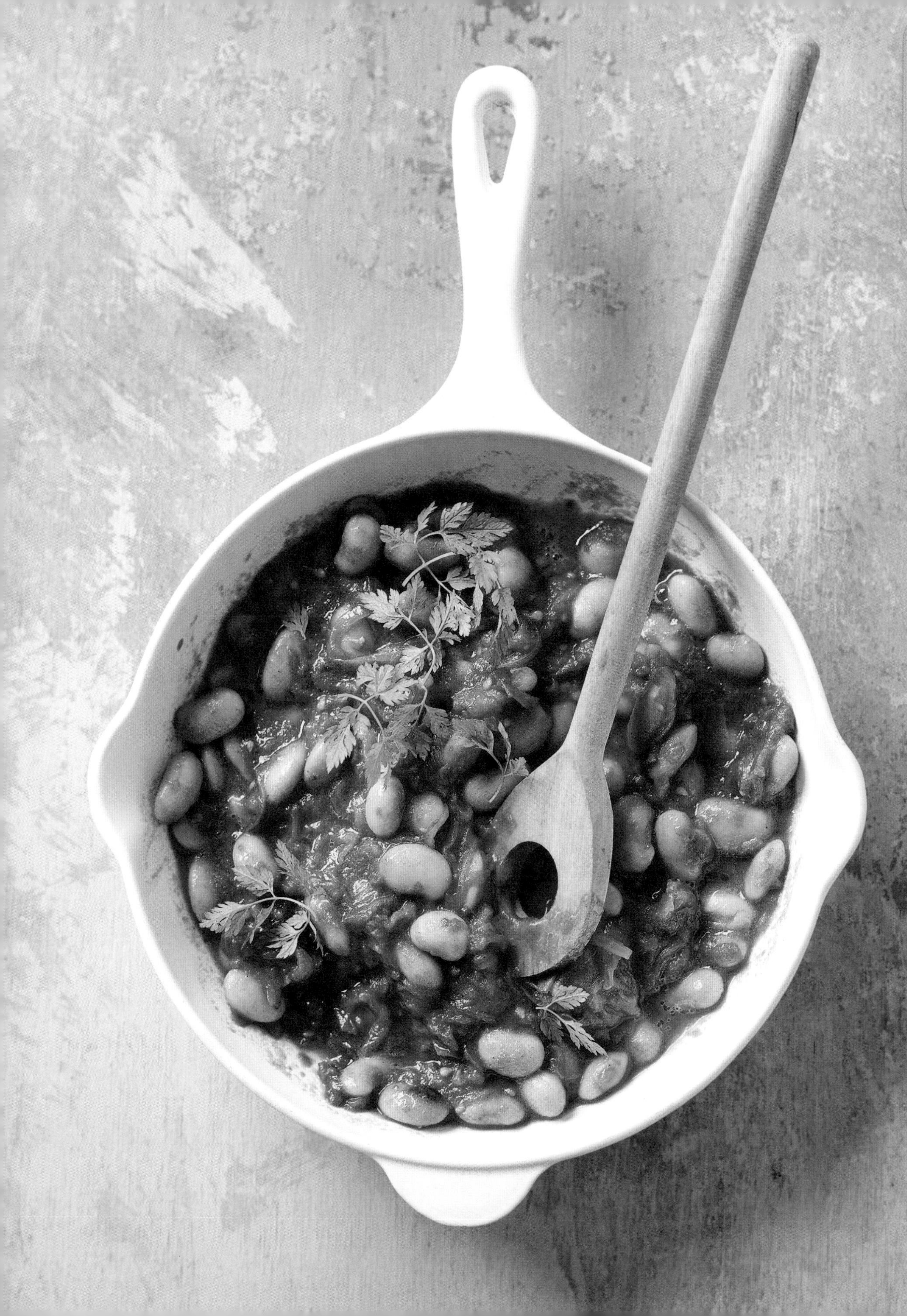

CARROT *and* COCONUT CHIA SEED PUDDING

SERVES 4

- 1 carrot, finely grated
- 1 cup white chia seeds
- 2 cups full-fat coconut milk
- ½ cup desiccated coconut
- ½ cup raw unsalted cashews
- 2 teaspoons vanilla extract
- 1 teaspoon ground cinnamon
- raspberries, to serve (optional)

This versatile pudding can be prepared in the evening to eat for breakfast or in the morning before work to eat for dessert. Carrots work beautifully in this recipe as they add a vibrant colour as well as sweetness, but if you are used to really sweet foods you could replace the carrot with an apple or pear until your tastebuds adjust. It's also easy to turn this into more of a dessert by serving berries on top; I like raspberries with carrot and blueberries with apple or pear. Get creative and find your own favourite combinations!

Combine all the ingredients with ½ cup of water and stir well. Divide among 4 small bowls or jars, allowing room for the mixture to swell by about one third.

Pop in the fridge overnight or before you leave for work and enjoy for breakfast or dessert with raspberries on top, if you like.

NOTE FROM DAMON:
FOR A BREAKFAST YOU CAN TAKE
ANYWHERE, POP THE MIXTURE
INTO JARS RATHER THAN BOWLS.
NO NEED TO BUY FANCY MASON
JARS UNLESS YOU WANT TO.
WE JUST KEEP OUR OLD PASTA
SAUCE AND PEANUT BUTTER JARS.
SCRAPE OFF THE LABELS, WASH
THEM OUT AND RECYCLE THEM.

VEGAN   LEFTOVERS   TODDLER FRIENDLY

TRAFFIC-LIGHT EGGS

SERVES 3–6

6 similar-sized capsicums:
2 green, 2 red, 2 yellow

1 cup grated cheddar

3 cups baby spinach, wilted

6 free-range eggs

I am all for re-introducing old-fashioned recipes that are simple and delicious. And these little retro beauties deserve a second life. Choose capsicums with even proportions that will help them balance on the tray. The red and yellow ones bring sweetness, while the green ones are more mellow.

These eggs are also delicious with a tablespoon of beef mince or some pesto. This is a great way to use up leftovers, as well as adding extra flavour.

Preheat the oven to 180°C and line a baking tray with baking paper.

Cut the tops off the capsicums and remove the membrane and seeds. Divide the grated cheese among the capsicums. Squeeze any excess liquid from the spinach and add it to the capsicums, then crack an egg on top of each one.

Place the filled capsicums on the prepared tray. Roast them for 20–30 minutes or until the eggs are puffed up and cooked through.

NOTE FROM DAMON:
TAKE NOTE OF THE
INCREDIBLE NATURAL
SWEETNESS OF ROASTED
CAPSICUMS – THEY ARE
PERFECT FOR BRIDGING WEEK.

VEGETARIAN   LEFTOVERS

GREEN PEA FRITTERS

SERVES 4

2 cups frozen peas, thawed

1 ripe avocado

1 free-range egg, beaten

2 teaspoons salt

½ cup coconut flour

butter, for frying

These easy fritters are sweet and light in taste while still being filling. Leftovers are perfect for lunch. Enjoy them with a side of bacon, sour cream or Cultured 'Cream Cheese' (see page 119).

Place half of both the peas and avocado in a food processor and blitz to a paste. In a large bowl, crush the remaining peas with the back of a fork or a masher, then add the remaining avocado and mash. Add the pea and avocado paste, the beaten egg and salt and stir to combine.

Add the coconut flour, a little at a time, sprinkling it over the top and folding it through.

Heat a large frying pan with a little butter over medium heat. Using slightly wet hands, scoop out golf-ball-sized portions of the fritter mixture and shape it into patties; you should end up with 8.

Working in batches, add the patties to the pan and fry gently for a few minutes, then flip over to fry the other side; you can pop a lid on to help them cook through. Serve immediately.

VEGETARIAN   LEFTOVERS   TODDLER FRIENDLY

FLUFFY OMELETTE

**SERVES 4
(OR 2 GENEROUSLY)**

6 free-range eggs

50 g goat's cheese, crumbled

1 tablespoon coconut oil

torn baby spinach, to garnish
(optional)

Trust me: I know this looks plain; but it really is the fluffiest, most delectable omelette you'll ever make – providing you follow the method correctly. It is so easy and so delicious. You can spice it up with some extra goat's cheese and chilli flakes sprinkled on top, or add some avocado on the side to make it extra hearty. Please give it a whirl – it deserves attention!

Beat the eggs together with a fork or beater until well combined and bubbles appear on the surface. Add the goat's cheese.

Heat a large frying pan over medium–high heat. Spoon the coconut oil into the frying pan and turn down the heat to medium. Once the oil has melted, tip in the eggs and place the (preferably transparent) lid on the pan immediately.

Watch closely: as the omelette starts to firm up and rise, give the pan a shake with the lid still on to loosen the omelette from the bottom (if you don't have a transparent lid, take a very quick peek). Once it has fully puffed up – after a few minutes – remove the lid.

Slice the omelette into halves or quarters and serve straight away. Garnish with torn baby spinach, if you like.

NOTE FROM DAMON:
I KNOW THIS SEEMS INCREDIBLY SIMPLE – AND MOST OF US KNOW HOW TO MAKE AN OMELETTE – BUT THIS ONE IS ALL ABOUT THE 'FLUFFING' TECHNIQUE.

VEGETARIAN   TODDLER FRIENDLY

SAVOURY BREAKFAST MUFFINS

MAKES 6

butter, for frying

6 bacon rashers,
roughly chopped

6 free-range eggs
(plus 1 extra, if needed)

2 teaspoons sumac

2 cups chopped spinach

1 cup sweetcorn

Just because you're lowering your sugar intake, you don't need to throw away your baking tins! Hold onto them and just switch the contents over from sweet to savoury. This is another recipe that is perfect for using up leftovers, and you can easily double the quantities to make extra muffins for lunch the following day.

I love using sumac in my recipes, so you'll notice it quite a bit in this book. This Middle Eastern spice adds a lemony flavour and lovely rusty red colour to a wide variety of dishes. Give it a try.

Preheat the oven to 180°C and line a 6-hole muffin tin with paper cases.

Heat a frying pan over medium heat and throw in a nub of butter. Add the bacon and fry for 3 minutes, stirring occasionally.

Meanwhile, beat the eggs and sumac together.

Add the spinach and corn to the frying pan with the bacon, and stir to combine for just a minute until the corn is warm and the spinach is wilted slightly but still bright green.

Spoon the bacon mixture into the muffin tray, then pour in the beaten egg to reach halfway up the side of each hole; you may need to beat an additional egg if your eggs are small.

Bake the muffins for 15–20 minutes or until they have puffed up and are firm to the touch.

LEFTOVERS   TODDLER FRIENDLY

HEARTY WARMING SALAD

SERVES 6

coconut oil, for cooking

500 g pumpkin, chopped into
2 cm cubes

500 g (about 2 small) sweet
potato, chopped into 2 cm cubes

1 teaspoon salt

2 teaspoons ground cumin

1 large orange

1 large pomegranate

1 × 400 g tin lentils (brown
or green), drained and rinsed

1 cup raw almonds

This is a great transitional recipe to serve when you're missing the 'sweet stuff'. The orange brings freshness; the pumpkin and sweet potato substance and earthiness; and the pomegranate seeds, texture and jewel-like sparkle. Enough to make anyone happy.

Preheat the oven to 180°C.

Scoop up some coconut oil with your hands and rub the pumpkin and sweet potato all over with the oil. Spread them out over a large baking tray. Sprinkle with the salt and cumin and work them over again with your hands. Get the tray into the oven and keep an eye on it while you prepare the other ingredients.

Finely grate about 1 tablespoon of orange zest into a large bowl. Peel the orange and cut the segments into pieces roughly the size and shape of your pumpkin cubes. Chuck the orange into the bowl.

Cut the pomegranate in half across its middle. Hold it over the bowl with the seeds facing your hand and, using the back of a wooden spoon, whack the skin firmly so the little jewels fall out into your hand and the bowl below. This is by far the easiest way to seed a pomegranate and once you try it you'll never look back. Add the lentils to the bowl too.

Once the pumpkin and sweet potato are tender in the middle and slightly crispy on the outside, about 40–45 minutes, remove them from the oven and allow to cool a little.

Roughly chop the almonds; it doesn't matter if some are left almost whole. Add the pumpkin and sweet potato to the rest of the salad ingredients in the bowl and mix them together. Scatter the almonds on top to serve.

VEGAN   LEFTOVERS

ZUCCHINI NOODLE PAD THAI

SERVES 4–6

2 large zucchini, spiralised or very thinly sliced

1 large carrot, spiralised or very thinly sliced

1 cup bean sprouts, trimmed

1 cup sliced radish

100 g firm tofu, cut into 2 cm dice

2 spring onions, white and green parts finely sliced

1 cup peanuts, soaked overnight in ½ cup water and ½ cup soy sauce, then drained

DRESSING

⅓ cup lime juice

⅓ cup soy sauce, tamari or Bragg All Purpose Seasoning (available from health food shops)

1 tablespoon peanut butter

1 date, pitted

2 teaspoons freshly grated ginger

1 tablespoon olive oil

Home cooking can be simple *and* spectacular, as this recipe proves. It's the kind of meal you order once in a restaurant and end up returning for time and again; it's that moreish. Plus, when you eat it, you feel like you're on holiday in Thailand. 'Nuff said.

Spiralisers seem to be everywhere at the moment. You don't absolutely need one for this recipe – you can always use a mandoline or a very sharp knife and lots of patience instead (insert yawn emoji). However, you can buy cheap pencil-sharpener-style spiralisers nowadays and they are really easy to use; I much prefer them to the cumbersome countertop winch-like ones.

You'll need to soak the peanuts the day before serving this salad, and you can always use the soaking water as the base of the dressing if you're feeling frugal. Keep the dressing and salad separate if you're storing leftovers for later, otherwise your veggies will become soggy.

. . . .

For the dressing, blend all the ingredients until smooth, adding up to ⅓ cup of water to thin the sauce, as needed.

Toss the zucchini, carrot, bean sprouts, radish, tofu, spring onion and peanuts together in a large serving bowl.

Serve with the dressing on the side.

VEGAN   LEFTOVERS

SPICED COCONUT VEGGIES

SERVES 6–8

2 cups desiccated coconut

1 cup raw unsalted peanuts
or cashews

½ cup crispy fried shallots
(available from Asian groceries)

½ banana, mashed with
a little coconut oil

½ cup melted coconut oil

2 cloves garlic, sliced

grated zest of 1 lime

juice of 2 limes

2 tablespoons soy sauce or tamari

1 small red chilli,
seeded and sliced (optional)

300 g green beans,
topped and tailed

200 g white cabbage, sliced

100 g bean sprouts

400 g baby spinach

sliced cucumber and lime wedges,
to serve

My father lives in Indonesia and I spent many school holidays there. As a result, I get cravings for Indonesian food from time to time. To get my fix, I cook my childhood favourites – sugar-free versions, of course. This recipe is a variation of a dish called *urap*. It ticks lots of boxes: it's very quick to make, keeps well for lunch the following day, and is absolutely delicious. My Indonesian step-mother, however, might have something to say about my loose interpretation of her classic dish!

Preheat the oven to 180°C.

Place the desiccated coconut, nuts, shallots, mashed banana, melted coconut oil, garlic, lime zest and juice, soy sauce and chilli (if using) in a large bowl and toss together to mix. Spread the mixture out over a large baking tray, then place in the oven for 10–15 minutes or until aromatic and a little crispy; give it a little shake halfway through cooking.

Bring a saucepan of water to the boil. Place the green beans and cabbage in a steamer set over the pan, and steam until just tender; you want them to still be vibrant and a little crunchy.

Arrange the steamed vegetables, bean sprouts and spinach on a large serving plate. Remove the spiced coconut from the oven and scatter it over the top. Serve with freshly sliced cold cucumber and lime wedges on the side.

VEGAN   LEFTOVERS

FEISTY MEXICAN FRITTATA

**SERVES 4 GENEROUSLY
OR 6 WITH A SIDE SALAD**

butter, for greasing and frying

1 teaspoon sumac

1 teaspoon ground cumin

½ teaspoon chilli powder
(optional)

1 large red onion, sliced

2 large red capsicums, sliced

1 large green capsicum, sliced

1 teaspoon salt

1 × 400 g tin pinto or black beans,
drained and rinsed

2 ripe tomatoes, sliced

5 free-range eggs, beaten

chopped flat-leaf parsley or
coriander, to serve

diced avocado, to serve

Coriander is the great herby divider. I am firmly in Camp Coriander, whereas Damon is definitely not! In my opinion, it makes a fantastic garnish for this frittata, especially with some fresh chilli, a squeeze of lime, some sour cream and a dollop of my Guacamole (see page 211). But if you're on Damon's team, a sprinkling of parsley works just as well.

Preheat the oven to 180°C and lightly grease a small baking dish.

Heat a large frying pan over medium heat and add a little butter. Add the sumac, cumin and chilli powder and warm for a minute to become fragrant, then add the onion, capsicum and salt. Turn the heat down to low and gently caramelise for 30 minutes. Add the beans for a brief moment before removing the pan from the heat.

Tip the contents of the pan into the prepared dish and lay slices of tomato over the top. Pour over the beaten egg. Pop in the oven for 30 minutes.

Garnish with parsley or coriander leaves or diced avocado and serve warm or cold.

NOTE FROM DAMON:
THERE SHOULD BE 'TEAM
CORIANDER' AND 'SAY NO
TO CORIANDER' T-SHIRTS.
I WOULD PROUDLY WEAR
THE LATTER.

VEGETARIAN   LEFTOVERS

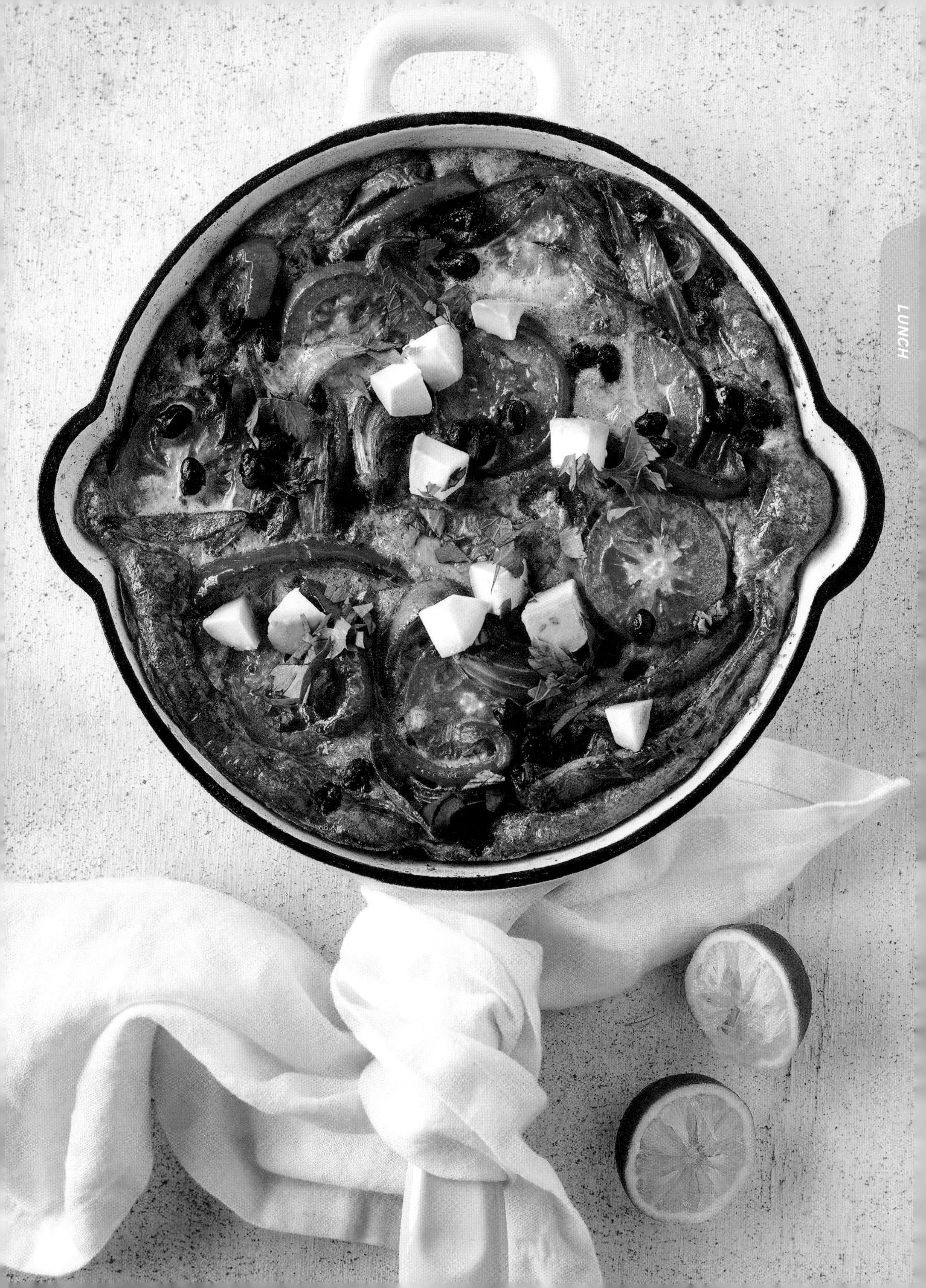

MUM'S HEARTY PEA *and* HAM SOUP

SERVES 4

500 g mixed dried beans and peas (soup mix) and/or frozen peas

butter, for frying

200 g speck (or a few smoky bacon bones or a smoked hock – even a few bacon rashers), cut into bite-sized pieces

1 clove garlic, chopped

1 onion or leek, finely sliced

2–3 cups chopped vegetables – a mixture of the following works nicely: carrots, turnips, parsnips, celery, broad beans, peas

good handful of chopped flat-leaf parsley and/or a few bay leaves

chopped flat-leaf parsley (extra), to serve

grated cheese, to serve (optional)

'There really is nothing better than Mumma's home cooking,' said everyone in every country in every language every day! My mum has been making this soup for as long as I can remember and we love it.

This hearty, warming soup is the ideal fare for a cold evening. It's easy to put together and infinitely adaptable with just three basic sets of ingredients: frozen peas or dried bean and pea mix; lots of vegetables; and some ham, bacon or bones with a smoky, meaty taste. What's more, it is the perfect recipe to cook when you are cleaning out the fridge. This recipe serves 4, but can be easily doubled.

• •

If you're using dried beans and peas, soak them in water overnight, then drain and rinse thoroughly. The longer the beans and peas soak for, the quicker they'll cook.

If you're using frozen peas, remove them from the freezer to thaw.

Melt the butter in a heavy-bottomed stockpot or saucepan over medium heat and throw in your speck or porky bits to brown and crisp for about 5 minutes, stirring occasionally. Turn the heat down to low and add the garlic and onion or leek, then the chopped vegetables and sweat them for 10 minutes until tender. Pour in 1 cup of water and bring to a simmer. Toss in your chosen beans and/or peas and stir. Poke the meat down and cover with water (or use vegetable stock, if you have some to hand). Add the herbs.

Bring to the boil, then turn down the heat, and mash the peas and veggies together with a potato masher so they are broken up but not completely pureed. Cover and stir occasionally to prevent the veggies from sticking to the bottom. The only thing that can go wrong with this soup is the liquid evaporating, which will make the mixture heavy, so keep an eye on it and be sure to add a little more water if needed.

The soup is ready when the peas are soft, the veggies have melted into a mush and the meat is falling off the bones, about 30 minutes. The final soup will be thick, like porridge. To serve, take out the bones, if necessary, and dollop the soup into bowls. Finish with a little extra parsley and some grated cheese if you like.

LEFTOVERS　TODDLER FRIENDLY　BABY FRIENDLY

MUSHROOM PATE *and* VEGGIE DIPPERS

SERVES 4–6

MUSHROOM PATE

100 g butter

700 g swiss brown or button mushrooms

1 tablespoon apple cider vinegar

100 g coconut oil

VEGGIE DIPPERS

1 large carrot

2 celery sticks

1 Lebanese cucumber

This pate proves surprisingly meaty for those who want to eat less meat but still enjoy the taste of meat. Is that a confusing sentence? Oh well. You'll work it out, I'm sure!

To make the mushroom pate, melt the butter in a frying pan over medium-high heat. Throw in the mushrooms and brown slightly for 2 minutes, then add the vinegar and continue to fry for a couple more minutes, until the mushrooms have shrunk slightly but are still firm. Scoop the coconut oil into the blender and pour the cooked mushrooms with their buttery juices over the top. Whizz together to form a smooth paste.

Slice all your veggies into batons and arrange on a plate for serving.

Serve the mushroom pate warm with your veggie dippers or transfer it to an airtight jar and leave in the fridge to set for a couple of hours. This should keep for up to 4 days in an airtight container in the fridge.

VEGETARIAN   LEFTOVERS   TODDLER FRIENDLY

LEFTOVER SAVOURY MUFFINS

MAKES 12 SMALL MUFFINS

200 g leftover corned beef
(page 89), roughly chopped

2 cups roughly chopped
vegetables (I like carrots,
celery and apple here)

4 free-range eggs

I've included this recipe to show you how easy it is to incorporate leftovers from other meals into a new dish. These muffins use up the leftover silverside from the recipe on page 89, but you could just as easily use leftovers from the Slow-cooked Coconut Chicken on page 190 or the veggies from the Gado Gado on page 92 with a tablespoon of peanut sauce. It's all about getting creative and reducing food waste by using up small amounts of leftovers before they end up in the bin.

Preheat the oven to 180°C and line a small 12-hole muffin tin with papers.

Pulse the meat and veg in a food processor for a minute, then crack in the eggs and pulse again for another couple of minutes.

Spoon a couple of tablespoons of the mixture into each muffin paper.

Bake for 15–20 minutes or until the muffins are slightly brown on top.

LEFTOVERS   TODDLER FRIENDLY   OCCASIONAL FOODS

CAULIFLOWER 'RICE' BALLS

SERVES 4 WITH A SIDE

1 large cauliflower

1 cup almond meal,
plus extra for dusting

3 free-range eggs, beaten

½ cup finely grated parmesan

1 teaspoon dried oregano

1 teaspoon paprika
(optional but delicious)

pepper, to taste

100 g mozzarella,
chopped into 2 cm cubes

olive oil, for spraying and
drizzling (optional)

baby spinach, to serve (optional)

lemon wedges, to serve (optional)

Our toddler *loves* these. Win for me – yay! She thinks anything ball-shaped is pretty fantastic, actually. So this is how my logic went when I created this recipe: toddlers like balls so if I turn food into balls, they might not just throw it, but eat it too!

I like eating these just by themselves for lunch – the cheese in the insides makes them deliciously saucy and filling – but these are also good served with a simple side dish (see pages 206–207 for ideas). You can easily adapt the method to make mini balls to serve as an appetiser or as snacks for children. You can also double this recipe to give you leftovers for lunch the following day.

. . . .

Preheat the oven to 180°C and line a baking tray with baking paper.

Hold the cauliflower head in your hand and slam the stem on a chopping board to break it into florets. You can steam them briefly at this stage, if you like, but I rarely bother. Chuck the florets into a food processor and pulse until the mixture resembles rice. Transfer to a bowl and add the almond meal, beaten eggs, parmesan, oregano, paprika and pepper. Combine well.

Sprinkle the chopping board with extra almond meal. Scoop up a tennis-ball-sized portion of the cauliflower mixture and shape with your hands to make it nice and round. Take a cube of mozzarella and, using your thumb or finger, press it into the centre of the cauliflower ball. Reshape the ball to cover the hole, then roll the ball gently in the almond meal to cover lightly. Set the cauliflower ball on the prepared tray and repeat with the rest of the mixture, to make 6–8 balls. Spray with some oil, if you like. Place in the oven and cook for 20–30 minutes or until crisp and golden.

Serve straight away with baby spinach leaves and lemon wedges, if you like, and a drizzle of olive oil.

VEGETARIAN   LEFTOVERS   TODDLER FRIENDLY

MUSHROOM BUN BEEF BURGERS

SERVES 4

8 very large (bun-sized) mushrooms

coconut oil, melted, for drizzling

500 g beef mince

1 free-range egg

1 tablespoon sumac

2 teaspoons salt

butter, for frying

200 g sliced cheddar (or your favourite cheese)

½ cup thickly sliced pickles

2 tomatoes, sliced

1 cup loosely packed chopped iceberg lettuce

These are a bit of fun. Clearly a mushroom doth not a bread roll make, but they look so cute, we can overlook the taste difference (which is surprisingly meaty in itself)!

This protein-packed burger can also be adapted for vegetarians. Simply replace the beef with the same amount of beans (I like to use kidney, pinto or navy) and crush them well with your hands to ensure the patties stay together.

Preheat the oven to 180°C and line a baking tray with baking paper. Drizzle the mushrooms lightly with coconut oil on both sides then place on the prepared tray and bake for 6–8 minutes or until tender.

Meanwhile, in a large bowl, combine the mince, egg, sumac and salt. Divide the mixture into four, then using your hands, shape each portion into a ball and press it down to form a patty; the patties will shrink a little during cooking so make sure they're slightly larger then the mushrooms you'll be using for the buns. Set aside on baking paper.

Melt some butter in a lidded frying pan over high heat and once it's sizzling, place a couple of patties in to cook. Pop the lid on the pan; this will help steam the patties and reduce the cooking time. After 2 minutes, remove the lid and flip the patties over, then pop the lid back on and cook for a further 2 minutes.

Remove the patties from the pan and place them on a baking tray. Repeat with the remaining patties. Arrange the cheese on top, then the pickles. Place the topped patties in the oven briefly for the cheese to melt.

Meanwhile, remove the stems from the mushrooms (you can save these for the Mushroom Pate recipe on page 82, if you like). Layer half the mushrooms with a cheese-covered patty, fresh tomato and lettuce, and top with the remaining mushrooms. Best devoured immediately!

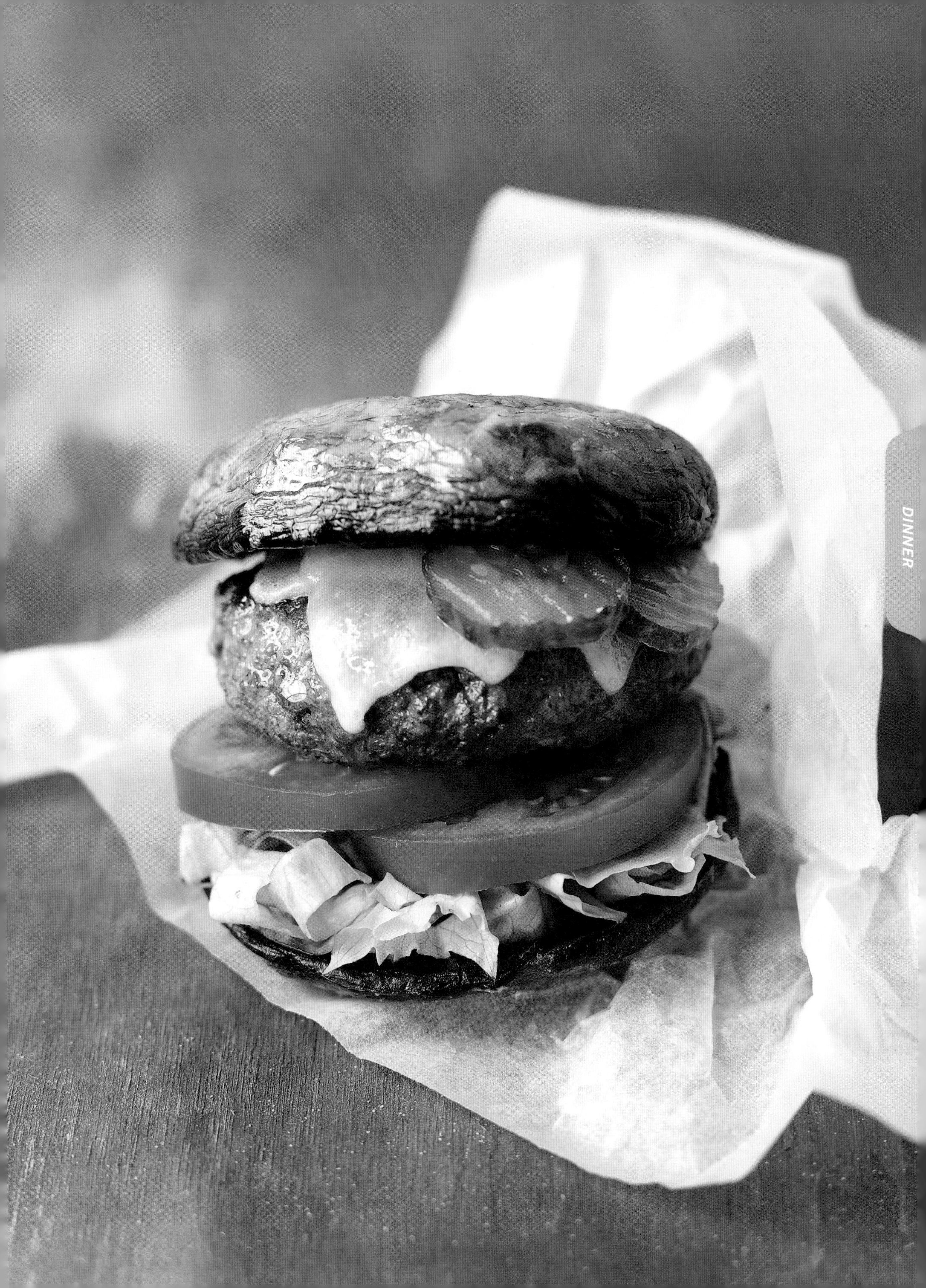

BAKED MINCE ZOODLES

SERVES 4

coconut oil, for greasing

4 long red capsicums, sliced in half, membrane and seeds removed

200 g fresh ricotta

1 large zucchini, spiralised

100 g parmesan, grated

SAUCE

butter, for frying

500 g beef mince

1 tablespoon ground cumin

juice of 1 lemon

500 g tinned crushed tomatoes

1 teaspoon salt

This recipe was a latecomer – we slipped it into the book at the last minute. I whipped this up in a hurry one night when we were all so tired from work and travel, and we needed something hearty and healthy, and fast. It more than hit the spot, surprising us with its deliciousness. (Sometimes those random experiments really are the best.) We ate it by itself as it contains a good balance of meat and veg, but you could bump it up with a green salad. We also enjoyed the leftovers for breakfast the next day!

Preheat the oven to 220°C and grease a baking dish (about 30 × 20 cm) with coconut oil.

For the sauce, melt some butter in a large frying pan over medium–high heat. Add the mince and allow it to brown for 3 minutes, stirring all the while to break it up and keep it browning evenly. Add the cumin and stir it through for a further 2 minutes. Squeeze the lemon juice over the mince and stir it for another minute, then add the tomatoes and salt, and stir to combine. Then pop on the lid and leave it to simmer for 15 minutes, stirring every 5 minutes or so. The resulting sauce should be fairly dry with just a bit of moisture.

Meanwhile, place the capsicum in one layer in the prepared baking dish and roast for 5–10 minutes to soften slightly; keep an eye on them to make sure they don't burn.

Remove the capsicum from the oven and layer half the mince sauce over the top, then half of the ricotta. Arrange the zucchini noodles on top. Add the remaining sauce, then the remaining ricotta. Top with the parmesan and return it to the oven for 15–20 minutes or until the top is crunchy and golden.

LEFTOVERS

GOOD OLE SILVERSIDE CORNED BEEF

SERVES 4–6

2 large carrots, trimmed and halved

3 celery sticks, trimmed and cut to the same size as the carrots

1 leek, trimmed and cut to the same size as the carrots

1 white sweet potato, rinsed well and halved

1 green apple, quartered

600 g silverside (corned beef), fat on

1 teaspoon whole black peppercorns

5 cloves

2 cinnamon sticks

2 bay leaves (optional)

1 tablespoon apple cider vinegar

This recipe is dear to my heart, as it was given to me by my late Great Aunty Val. One Christmas, at the age of 92, she cooked up a feast for 10 people; on Boxing Day we enjoyed the most mouthwatering silverside I have ever eaten, served with homemade mayo and leftovers from the day before. I will always remember her orange floral slow-cooker and the smell of the silverside bubbling away overnight in the laundry! (As she told me, 'It's the place to do your slow-cooking, dear, to keep the smell from permeating your kitchen.') Aunty Val's original recipe contained a little sugar, which I've replaced with apple here.

The memory of Aunty Val's health, vitality and love of good food and cooking stay with me to this day, and every time I prepare this dish I give a nod to the past generations of strong, capable women. This recipe may not be groundbreaking, but it's a truly delicious dish that deserves to be cooked in laundries around the world!

You can either use a slow cooker or an casserole dish for this. If you are using the latter, preheat the oven to 180°C.

Throw all the veggies and the apple into your slow cooker or casserole dish. Place the meat on top, then add the peppercorns, cloves, cinnamon and bay leaves (if using). Pour in the vinegar and enough water to cover the meat (about 1.5 litres).

If you are using the oven, reduce the temperature to 130°C and cook for 6 hours. If you are using a slow cooker, choose a low setting for 10–12 hours, or a higher setting for 5–6 hours.

Serve the silverside with the veggies and broth on the side. Alternatively, you can strain the broth and freeze it to use as stock. The meat can be stored in an airtight container in the fridge to use in salads or a lettuce cup sandwich. You can also use up leftovers in the Savoury Muffins on page 83.

LEFTOVERS   OCCASIONAL FOODS

SHAKE 'N' BAKE CHICKEN DRUMMIES

SERVES 4

8 chicken drumsticks

2 tablespoons coconut oil

⅓ cup finely grated parmesan

⅓ cup chia seeds

⅓ cup almond meal

1 tablespoon lemon thyme leaves

1 tablespoon sumac

This recipe is a fun, safe way to get kiddies involved in the kitchen. You can give them each their own paper bag and let them shake away! If you dare, you could even offer them some different spices to experiment with and come up with their own flavour combos. These are also great served with Easy Cheesy Cabbage Bake (see page 188).

Preheat the oven to 180°C and place a wire rack over a roasting tin.

Wash and pat dry the chicken drumsticks – dry them really well as this will create the crispy skin. Lather them in the coconut oil.

Put the parmesan, chia seeds, almond meal, thyme and sumac in a paper bag and give it a little shake to mix them together.

Working two at a time, place the chicken drumsticks in the paper bag and give them a good shake around until they are nicely coated. Place on the wire rack over the roasting tin and repeat with the remaining drumsticks.

Pop them in the oven and roast for 35 minutes or until the juices run clear when tested with a skewer.

GADO GADO *or* CHICKEN SATAY

SERVES 4

PEANUT SAUCE

2 dates, pitted and chopped

½ cup coconut oil

2 cups raw unsalted peanuts

2 cloves garlic, sliced

2 tablespoons soy sauce, tamari or Bragg All Purpose Seasoning

1 small red chilli, seeded (optional)

2 tablespoons lime juice

½ cup crispy fried shallots (available from Asian groceries)

GADO GADO

4 free-range eggs

1 small sweet potato, chopped

coconut oil, for frying

200 g tempeh or firm tofu, cut into thick slices

2 tablespoons soy sauce or tamari

200 g green beans, trimmed

200 g white cabbage, chopped

200 g baby spinach

100 g bean sprouts (optional)

1 Lebanese cucumber, sliced (optional)

CHICKEN SATAY

200 g chicken thigh fillets, chopped into 2 cm pieces

coconut oil, for cooking

Holiday food cooked at home! My Indonesian step-mother is a fantastic cook so I have eaten my fair share of satay and gado gado and, over the years, I have worked on perfecting my peanut sauce! The recipe here can be used for both the chicken satay and the gado gado. Traditionally, palm sugar is added, but I have used dates to sweeten the sauce.

The Indonesian street vendors, who cook the skewers over coals, chop the chicken into small cubes and I like it this way too. One last thing: remember to soak the skewers in water for 20 minutes before using them to prevent them from burning.

To make the peanut sauce, soak the dates in 1 cup of warm water for 2 hours. Melt the coconut oil in a large frying pan over medium heat. Fry the peanuts until toasted, about 7 minutes. At the last minute, add the garlic, then the soy and chilli (if using). Set aside to cool. Tip the peanuts into a food processor, along with the lime juice and dates and soaking water. Whizz to form a slightly coarse paste; add up to 1 cup of water to reach your desired consistency.

To make gado gado, fill a large saucepan with water and add the eggs and sweet potato. Place over high heat and bring to the boil. Set a timer for 15 minutes for the eggs and then remove them; cook the sweet potato for a further 15 minutes, then remove. Leave the saucepan of water on the heat.

Meanwhile, melt coconut oil in a large frying pan over medium heat and add the tempeh or tofu with a splash of soy. Let it brown for 2 minutes on one side before turning it to brown on the other. Remove from the heat. Place a large steamer or colander over the saucepan of still-boiling water. Steam the beans for 10 minutes until just tender, then remove. Lightly steam the cabbage for 7 minutes, then remove. Finally, wilt the spinach.

For the chicken satay, thread the chicken onto two-thirds of each wooden skewer. These are best cooked on the barbie until the meat is white and a little juice runs clear, but you can also use a frying pan. Cook for 10 minutes, turning until brown all over.

Shell the eggs and cut them in half. Arrange them on a plate with the sweet potato, fried tofu or tempeh, steamed vegetables, bean sprouts and cucumber, if using. Arrange the cooked skewers on a serving plate and pour the peanut sauce sprinkled with shallots over the top.

LEFTOVERS

COCONUT FISH FINGERS with PARSNIP CHIPS

SERVES 4

lemon or lime wedges, to serve

PARSNIP CHIPS

400 g small parsnips, peeled and quartered lengthways

butter, for roasting

1 teaspoon salt

FISH FINGERS

600 g whiting fillets, scaled and filleted, skin on

1 cup macadamias

2 cups coconut flour

2 eggs, lightly beaten

butter, for frying

This simple adaptation of a traditional crumb recipe is made with coconut flour, and it is so light and fresh. If whiting isn't available, another firm white fish will do; I suggest snapper or flathead tails, trimmed to size.

Preheat the oven to 160°C and line a baking tray with baking paper.

Spread the parsnips out over the prepared tray and use your hands to cover them with butter and salt. Pop them in the oven and keep an eye on them as they cook; after about 20 minutes they should be perfectly golden and a little crispy.

Rinse the fish fillets and pat them dry with paper towel. Cut them into fingers about 2 cm wide.

Put the macadamias in a food processor and pulse until the nuts are finely ground. Add the coconut flour and pulse for another minute. Transfer to a plate. Dip the fish pieces in the egg then the macadamia crumb. Set them aside on a plate or chopping board.

Melt the butter in a large frying pan over low–medium heat. Add the fish in batches, making sure you don't overcrowd the pan, and gently fry it for 2–3 minutes on each side until the crumb starts to turn golden. Remove from the pan and drain on paper towel, then repeat with the remaining fish. Serve immediately with parsnip chips and lemon or lime wedges.

> **NOTE FROM DAMON:**
> PARSNIPS ARE OFTEN AVOIDED BECAUSE OF THEIR GI SCORE OF 98 – BUT THIS IS MISLEADING AS THEY ACTUALLY HAVE A LOW GLYCEMIC LOAD (10), AS WELL AS BEING SUPER-HIGH IN FIBRE. THEY BELONG TO THE SAME PLANT FAMILY AS CELERY, PARSLEY AND CARROTS.

the
CONSOLIDATION
PHASE

the CONSOLIDATION PHASE

Now that the first week or so has passed, you should be starting to notice a few changes. Maybe you feel less foggy-headed, or a recurrent ache has dulled a little, or a layer of your 'hibernation suit' has melted away. Or maybe you have a cracking headache, long for a Tim Tam, and believe I am an A-grade wanker?

The good news is that, for most of you, this is the toughest part of the process. Hopefully, all sorts of microscopic chemical reactions are now taking place in your mouth cave and your sweet cravings are not as powerful as they were when you first opened this book.

More importantly, you might have started to regulate your appetite again. That's because of a very important hormone called leptin, which communicates with the part of your brain called the hypothalamus and has serious chats with serious consequences. The hypothalamus controls a number of vital functions in our body: it is like an airport control tower overseeing the flight paths of body temperature, hunger, thirst and fatigue. However, studies have shown that fructose interferes with the lines of communication between leptin and the hypothalamus, in particular, the signal released from our fat cells that tells us when we are full. Yes, the airport control tower loses contact with Air Satiety and trouble can ensue.

When I met the delightful Dr Kathleen Page at the University of Southern California, she told me about her experiments in which two separate groups were given either a glucose or fructose solution. While the glucose solution lit up the hypothalamus and alerted the body to feeling full, the fructose solution failed to register. You see, fructose enters the body like an undercover spy plane from a Bond film. This is why you could have a can of soft drink with a 'Happy Meal' and still feel hungry, or why downing a juice with breakfast was an easy thing to do. Emphasis on *was*. Because hopefully you have noticed yourself feeling fuller throughout the day now that you are eating less sugar. Replacing the sugar with healthy fats and fibre (in whole fruits and vegetables especially) will also help the satiety process. It's like installing high-speed broadband between leptin and the hypothalamus control tower. You will feel less inclined to eye off the sesame snaps at 3:30 in the afternoon.

The next set of recipes (starting on page 147) is designed to consolidate your new way of eating. They are real foods free from added sugar. Now your body can start doing all the things it is naturally so good at, like regulating appetite and using the liver in its full capacity. It has probably been hanging out to do this for a long time while you were obliviously dropping fructose bombs into it.

YOUR SUPERMARKET SURVIVAL GUIDE

Over the past 20 years, since leaving the maternal nest and having the responsibility of grocery shopping thrust upon me, I have often enjoyed a gentle stroll around the supermarket. The colours are bright and the music is serene, and I usually leave with a whistling gait, knowing that the 'lasting-til-infinity' plastic bags embedded into my fingers and cutting off my blood supply contain adequate fuel to get me through the week. (Since the arrival of the wonderful Zoe, I now take canvas bags. A tick for the planet *and* for my fingers.)

But as much as I enjoyed making *That Sugar Film*, I also learnt many things I can sadly never un-learn. So here I am going to impart those sneaky tricks of the trade used by supermarkets to cunningly lure you into more purchases. Consider this your supermarket survival guide.

My insider knowledge comes predominantly from two terrific books, *Why We Buy: The Science of Shopping* by Paco Underhill and *Buyology: Truth and Lies About Why We Buy* by Martin Lindstrom. Underhill found that 60–70 per cent of purchases made at the supermarket were unplanned. This number was highest if the shopper came to the store by car instead of on foot (the shopper being mindful of how much they had to carry home).

It should come as no surprise that supermarkets very cheekily orchestrate their space to make you scan more items on the way out, leading to more 'beeps' at the checkout, which translate to more 'kerchings' in the bank. Here are some tips to help you navigate the fluorescent, pan-piped food cauldrons:

- Breads and baked goods are often placed near the front entrance. The alluring smells trigger salivary glands and activate the brain so you are in more of a 'mood to buy food'. They are also high-margin goods that need to be sold or they'll be thrown out, thus the supermarket needs them to cast their spell on you when your basket is empty and you are fresh and ready to shop.

- With that in mind, don't go shopping hungry! Sounds simple but it's amazing how your choices will be affected if your tummy is rumbling and your blood sugars are down. You will be lured into rows of those sweet-smelling breads and other refined carbohydrates. Enter the supermarket cage match feeling calm and centred. You've got this.

- Essentials like milk and eggs are often placed at the rear of the store so you have to pass many enticing goodies along the way (it could be the loading bays are also at the back of the store but that in no way suits our tone).

- The music is often calm and relaxing. A study by Nicolas Gueguen revealed people will stay longer if the music is soothing and they don't feel hurried. The study also showed that people buy more expensive items when classical music is played. Perhaps wearing headphones and making an upbeat 'shopping mix' will help. Personally, I find a grindcore mega-mix gets the shopping done in 10 minutes.

Real estate is key and companies jostle for the position of optimum eye-level height. I have seen footage of customers walking around with cameras on their heads so researchers can see where their eyes commonly go. These spots become the Mayfair and Park Lane of the Shopopoly money-making game. In the 1990s Coca Cola even went to the extremes of releasing a cheaper-brand cola just to fill up the space around its hero product. This ensured other high-profile competitors couldn't claim the space and thus pull focus from it. Children's eye level is also a much sought-after space, especially for cartoon-themed sweetened cereals.

Even the size of the shopping trolley counts. Research has found that consumers bought 40 per cent more when the trolley size was doubled.

Stores also often swap the aisles around. This means you can't just head straight for your product in its usual spot – you have to search for it and thus walk past other temptations. This is really bloody cheeky. Rearranging the shelving! Inducing Alzheimer's to make money.

Some stores deliberately use red stickers for prices. This is because we associate red with discounts so will be inclined to reach for that option.

If eye-level space is the Mayfair of Shopopoly, then the shelf space at the checkouts is like owning hotels on red, yellow and green. These carefully crafted pockets bedazzle the listless shopper who is waiting in line for their turn on the conveyer belt. In those moments, the victim is devoid of something to do, vulnerable and alone, perhaps a bit awkward. It is here that the comforting candy show awaits, alongside the gossip magazines with their promise of botoxed companionship and health secrets.

When research revealed 60 per cent of shoppers offloaded a product at the checkout after second thoughts, some stores reduced this space so there were fewer places to 'dump the load'.

NAVIGATING THE SUPERMARKET GAME

MILK + EGGS ZONE

FROZEN FOOD ZONE

FRUIT ZONE

VEGETABLE ZONE

BREAD

CEREAL

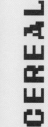

START HERE

 # MEAT ZONE

BISCUIT ZONE

SAUCE ZONE

SOFT DRINK ZONE

CHECK OUT ZONE

But before you lament or even develop some kind of supermarket anxiety disorder – Aldiphobia? Woolwarts? Coles-sores? – here is the magnificent and incredibly simple antidote (and it's not headphones)…

WRITE A SHOPPING LIST!

It may not seem much, but this list of carefully constructed food items will be your protective shield against the marketing tricks and ploys. It will gently lull you away from the shiny lights and bargain bins and softly whisper, 'Come back to me, you are safe here. I have everything you need'.

(I just had an image of supermarkets full of headphone-wearing humans hunched over shopping lists, pinching their noses to avoid alluring smells and terrified to look up. Please don't do that.)

Your shopping list will be like a map, guiding you efficiently through the rugged corporate terrain. You could even turn it into a game with the kids, sending them off on missions to find the lowest-sugar varieties of what they want.

Understanding is key and once you know the supermarket tricks being used, you will be able to spot them, have a little chuckle to yourself and then make a beeline for the fresh produce aisle. Soon enough new habits will form and these new habits will see your health and wellbeing dramatically improve.

LOOK AT ME!

Shopping List

We have listed these real-food ingredients in a lift-out poster in this book. Consider it a genuine food-porn centrefold. It's a terrific starting guide to buying real food again. It will look great on your fridge too.

* **FRUIT AND VEGETABLES:**
Buying seasonal produce will keep the costs down. Your level of fruit intake will depend on a number of factors like metabolic health, weight and levels of exercise, but try and keep the high sugar fruits like mangoes and grapes to occasional treats (especially if you are insulin sensitive). The current Australian recommendations are for two serves of whole fruit a day.

* **HEALTHY FATS:**
Avocados, nuts, olive oil, cheese (aged cheddar), eggs, fish, chia seeds, full-fat organic yoghurt

* **PROTEINS:**
Eggs, meat, beans, fish, lentils, chickpeas, tempeh, edamame (soy beans), quinoa, nuts, cheese

* **WHOLEGRAINS:**
Read the grains section if you haven't already (see page 49). These should be used very rarely during the transition but are okay to introduce in small amounts when you feel you are in good health.

* **DAIRY** (if it's your thing):
Full-fat organic yoghurt, cheese, full cream (with berries) as a treat. We have also recently discovered nutritional yeast flakes, which make a terrific alternative to cheese if you don't deal with dairy.

* **FOODS FOR EMERGENCY CRAVINGS**
> A teaspoon of coconut oil, husk or cream
> A handful of nuts (almonds, macadamia, cashews)
> A small bowl of full-fat plain yoghurt with some frozen blueberries
> Dried coconut flakes (with no added sugar)
> A teaspoon of avocado
> A small smoothie with half an avocado, half a banana, ¼ cup of coconut milk and water
> Something you really don't like the taste of, such as apple cider vinegar (reverse psychology)
> A small glass of kombucha (see page 115)

EATING REAL FOODS CHEAPLY

One of the real surprises of making *That Sugar Film* was how little my expenditure on food changed before and during the high-sugar experiment. This is because when I was eating all the low-fat foods and refined carbohydrates for the filming madness, I rarely felt full so I needed to snack more, which meant I needed to spend more. When I returned to my diet of real foods with fibre and healthy fats, the appetite controls returned, I felt fuller for longer throughout the day and, although I paid a little more for the goods, I bought less so it worked out roughly the same. I am also very confident that I'm saving myself some medical bills in the future.

There is no denying that some processed foods are cheaper than real foods and I hope that I see this change in my lifetime. But while we wait for the paradigm shift, there are some ways you can save money and still nourish yourself.

✓ **Write that shopping list:** This is vital for a number of reasons. If you stick to the shopping list, you won't be seduced by other items at the supermarket – you will shop efficiently and save cashish.

✓ **Buy seasonal:** Often the fruits and veggies that are out of season are much more expensive. Consult Dr Google to find out what's in season, and therefore more likely to be abundant and cheap.

✓ **Buy veg and fruit in bulk when it's on sale and then freeze it:** My stepmother does this with trays of mangoes when they go on sale and it's so fantastic to eat a mango in winter for a change.

✓ **Buy frozen if you need to:** We purchase a bag of frozen blueberries with every shop. They're even better when you pour a bit of cream on top and the cream solidifies. Delicious. Frozen fish gets an occasional workout too (I don't recommend pouring cream on frozen fillets though).

✓ **Preparation for the week:** Try to prepare some meals for the week when you get home from shopping. Make some large dishes and then freeze what you don't have for dinner for lunches or another dinner a few nights later. Soups and stews are winners here.

Grow your own herbs: A windowsill or a few pots on the back patio will do. They are so much cheaper and have great flavour, plus you'll be rewarded with a good feeling when you add your own home-grown herbs to a meal. We have recently branched out to growing our own kale and lettuce. So far the snails are getting the most benefits.

Have a large, nourishing breakfast: I always try to get some eggs and healthy fats in early that will last me all the way to lunch. I might pack some nuts and cheese or fruit for an emergency, but usually find that breakfast will last me a few hours and save me spending money on a mid-morning snack.

Don't be fooled by pre-made salad mixes: Make your own; it might take longer but you will get much more bang for your buck.

Buy a whole chook: While the pre-cut thighs and fillets look good and save time, you are better off buying the whole bird and dividing it yourself. The freezer is also your friend here.

Fall in love with beans: Some people may not be able to tolerate them, but we soak them first and find they are a brilliant, cheap way to fill out a meal. They are also packed with protein and microbiome-helping fibre (see page 112).

Check your pantry: Zoe and I regularly make the call that we have to use up the items in the pantry before our next shop. There is always a random can of beans or a bag of something lurking in the shadows of the cupboard or fridge. Make sure it gets put to use.

Canned fish is your friend: Zoe is a sucker for it. I often end up with a knock to the head from some kind of can falling when I open the cupboard door because they are stacked so high. A great source of protein and an incredibly versatile addition to meals.

Snack while you are shopping: Don't ever do this. Don't ever take a handful of nuts or grapes from the supermarket as you walk around. Don't ever pick at macadamias or expensive cheese. I did this once and boy did I cop the wrath of former-prefect Zoe. Rightly so: I stole. Sorry, Coles.

VEGETARIAN OPTIONS

You might notice we've included lots of vegetarian recipes in this book. This is due to a recent and staggering report from the Worldwatch Institute that showed 51 per cent of greenhouse emissions came from the meat industry (compared with 14 per cent from transport). This includes not only the methane produced by animals but actions like the clearing of rainforests to plant crops to feed the cattle. We still enjoy meat, but have certainly reduced our intake since researching this topic in more detail. It would make an enormous difference to the planet if we all just ate a little bit less bovine and other creatures.

ZOE

I was vegetarian for a few years in my twenties, prior to meeting Damon. It was an ethical stance that agreed with me and one I still have huge respect for, although I no longer practise it. The treatment of animals in the food industry, during their lives and in the way they're killed, has been found to be inhumane in many circumstances. Also, the effect of meat production on a mass scale and the amount of greenhouse gas it creates is severely damaging our planet.

Giving up meat altogether is just not an option for many people. However, we can try to eat it mindfully, with awareness of what we partake in. At home, Damon and I opt for biodynamic or organic animal products as much as possible (this applies to eggs, butter and cheese as well as meat). This can be expensive but it is our choice to invest in those who are commit-

ted to ethical practices. If this means we eat half the quantity of meat half as often, we are fine with that. When we are dining with friends and family, we are flexible and eat what we are offered. If we have a choice and find ourselves in a situation where we know the livestock was handled very poorly, we usually choose a vegetarian option. It's really about making ethical choices, within your budget, as much as possible. Begin small and see how you go. Every choice we make is about being increasingly aware of the whole picture, not just our own needs.

There are lots of veggie recipes in this book and if you need to modify vegetarian recipes for a vegan, this is easily done by substituting dairy for coconut oil and coconut products. Nutritional yeast flakes are also an amazing cheese replacement.

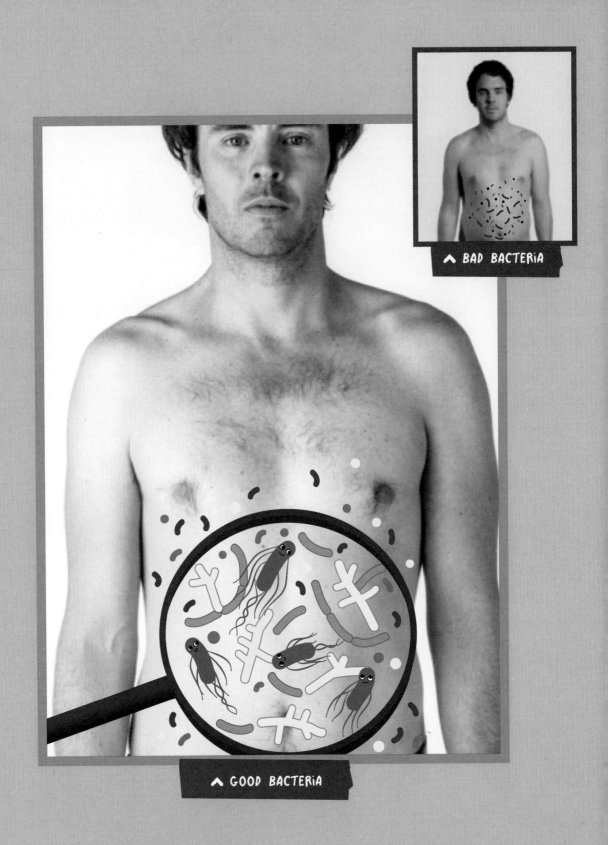

▲ BAD BACTERIA

▲ GOOD BACTERIA

SUGAR *and* GUT BACTERIA

Another motivating force for cleansing yourself of sugar and eating real foods is the exciting new research emerging about gut bacteria and the world of the microbiome. Our body is made up of 100 trillion microscopic bacteria called microbes (not to be confused with clothes for microphones). They can be found in the gut, the skin and all over the body. They are like a bustling metropolis of miniature organisms using your body as their planet. When we are born and pass along the birth canal we take many of these microbes from our mother, and experts are now telling us that these little microbes play a pivotal role in determining our health and immunity. In fact, they may even have protective qualities from conditions such as asthma, ADHD, obesity and type 1 diabetes.

There is good bacteria that help the body, but there is also bad bacteria. When you eat processed foods low in natural fibre and high in sugar and unhealthy fats (like trans fats), you create bad gut bacteria, and when you eat real foods with lots of fibre (like whole fruits, vegetables and nuts), you create good gut bacteria. Evidence also suggests that the amount of antibiotics you take, or did take as a child, will influence the world of the microbiome: antibiotics are a bit like a nuclear bomb dropped onto their planet.

Experiments have shown that microbe replacement therapy in the gut can have extraordinary outcomes on a range of conditions (they literally do a faecal transplant and take the bacteria from one person or mouse and implant it into another). There is evidence that these microbes in the gut can also have an influence on our brain and how we think and operate. Now you can see why there is a little bit of excited wee coming out of many scientists around the world who are researching this topic!

Again, this type of research continues to point to the healing power of real food, something we have always known but have recently forgotten or have been made to forget with the avalanche of marketing power. For many people, the world of the microbiome and gut bacteria may be the missing part of the puzzle as to why they continue to struggle with their weight or other health issues. There's lots more investigating to do but upping your real food and fibre intake certainly isn't going to hurt while we're waiting.

HIGH-FIBRE FOODS

The bad bacteria just loves sugar and refined carbohydrates, but once you stop feeding them they will no longer thrive. And conversely, a really important way of maintaining good bacteria or even restoring them is by eating high-fibre foods. Here's a list of some of the best:

WHITE, BLACK AND KIDNEY BEANS	PEARS	BROCCOLI
	RASPBERRIES	PARSNIPS
EDAMAME (SOY BEANS)	BLUEBERRIES	BRUSSELS SPROUTS
CHIA SEEDS	AVOCADOS	CARROTS
ALMONDS	ARTICHOKES	SPINACH
ORANGES	PEAS	

'Here's why fibre is so important to intestinal flora: your microbes feed on it and produce short-chain fatty acids, which get absorbed into the bloodstream and regulate the immune system and attenuate inflammation. That means if you're not eating dietary fibre, your immune system may be existing in kind of a simmering pro-inflammatory state.'

– **JUSTIN L. SONNENBURG, PHD, CO-AUTHOR OF** *THE GOOD GUT: TAKING CONTROL OF YOUR WEIGHT, YOUR MOOD, AND YOUR LONG-TERM HEALTH*

RECIPES TO HELP YOUR MICROBIAL WORLD

For those of you who may have already done some damage or are only now coming off a very high-sugar diet, you may need more than just high-fibre foods. It is important to invite some healing probiotics onto the microbiome dance floor. These can come in the form of supplements but also in food and drinks like kombucha, fermented vegetables, cultured yoghurt and apple cider vinegar. I often had a small side of fermented vegetables during my post-experiment cleanse, the 'kryptonite' to bad bacteria. It was a little confronting at first but I grew to enjoy the flavour.

Here are some terrific recipe ideas from Zoe to help you out.

Carrot Pop (see page 117)

HOME-BREWED KOMBUCHA

This is a great way to use up the last of the sugar in your house. Kombucha uses sugar to ferment, which means the sugar is 'eaten' up by the good bacteria as it grows. The longer it is left, the more vinegary it becomes and the better it is for you.

This is not an exact science, as the fermentation process is affected by so many factors including the quality of the original 'mother' or 'symbiotic colony of bacteria and yeast (SCOBY)' as well as the temperature of the room and the tea used. There are many variables. Experiment and learn through trying different methods.

Any mother will know that when you're growing your baby all you want to do is eat! Well, that's what the SCOBY is doing. Eating, specifically, the sugar. It uses this to grow more healthful bacteria, which are good for your gut; you can think of this as its baby. Basically the 'mother' is the strange-looking alien slime in your kombucha brew. This slime is your friend.

Kombucha should be brewed in a glass or ceramic container, not metal or plastic. It needs good filtered water to grow optimally, as tap water contains chemicals that kill bacteria, both good and bad indiscriminately.

The easiest way to start your own culture with a 'mother' is by going to the local organic store, buying a bottle of unpasteurised kombucha with the mother sediment in the bottom and growing a mother from this yourself.

1 bottle of unpasteurised kombucha

1 teaspoon sugar

Pour the kombucha into a large open-mouthed jar or bowl. Add a teaspoon of sugar. Cover it with a muslin cloth (I use our daughter's old baby muslin wraps) and leave it in an undisturbed, dark place at room temperature for a week. I often put ours in the back of our wine-glass cupboard as being rare drinkers we don't disturb those often! Check after a week and you should see a 'mother' has formed on top.

This is now ready to use along with some of the existing kombucha in your first ferment . . .

FIRST FERMENT: *the* MOTHER

2 litres filtered water

3 caffeinated organic tea bags
(you can use green or black tea
but it must be caffeinated)

⅓ cup sugar

1 kombucha mother
plus ½ cup of its liquid

Bring a litre of water to the boil. Remove it from the heat and pour it into a large open-mouthed receptacle – a large jar or bowl will do. Add the tea bags and leave them to steep until the brew has cooled to room temperature. Now remove the tea bags and add the sugar, stirring it to dissolve. Lastly, add the mother and the liquid from the previous batch. Cover the bowl with a clean muslin cloth and leave it in a dark place for a week to allow it to ferment.

After a week, check on your kombucha. You should see a cloudy, rubbery film over the top, which is the formation of the new mother. Try a little of the liquid and see if it is still sweet or has started turning vinegary. Ideally you want it to be quite tart as this means the sugar is mostly dissolved. If it's hot, this will have happened fast but if it's been cool it can take a little longer, say between 10 and 15 days. If it's too sweet, recover it and continue to ferment it for another week or so. If it's good and tart, then it's ready for the second ferment . . .

SECOND FERMENT: *the* FIZZ

CARROT POP

⅓ cup grated carrot

1 teaspoon grated ginger

APPLE SPIDER

1 small apple, sliced

BLUEBERRY BUCHA

½ cup blueberries

VANILLA

1 teaspoon vanilla extract

1 teaspoon raw honey (the honey,
like the sugar, will be consumed
in the fermentation process)

Gently scoop out the mother and ½ cup of its liquid and set aside in a jar to start your next batch of ferments. Pour your kombucha liquid into a glass bottle with an airtight pop top or cork. The bottle should be of good quality as the glass will be under pressure from the build-up of carbonation. Make sure it is only two-thirds full, otherwise you may need a second bottle. You're now ready to add your second ferment flavours to it. Here are some suggestions on the left:

It is best to start with a short second ferment of 2–4 days depending on the weather. If it's hot, try 2; if cooler, try 4. The risk you take here in leaving it longer is too much CO_2 building up and the carbonation causing the bottle to explode! So start by playing it safe, even if it's less fizzy, and then gradually get bolder as you get your techniques down.

After the 2–4 days, pop your brew in the fridge to cool it for another 24 hours before opening it and giving it a try. You can keep it in the fridge indefinitely.

VEGETARIAN

CULTURED 'CREAM CHEESE'

OLD-FASHIONED SAUERKRAUT

CULTURED 'CREAM CHEESE'

150 g plain organic Greek-style yoghurt or sheep's yoghurt

Pour the yoghurt into a muslin cloth. Tie it into a ball with an elastic band and drape it over a wooden spoon suspended over a glass bowl (or you can leave the muslin and yoghurt in a sieve placed over a bowl).

Leave it at room temperature overnight.

After this time, some liquid will have dripped into the bowl; the yoghurt in the muslin should have formed a firmer ball the consistency of cream cheese.

Unwrap the muslin and tip the 'cream cheese' out into an airtight container or bowl. Keep it in the fridge to use as you would cream cheese.

Meanwhile, leave the liquid (the whey) in the bowl and set aside to use for making sauerkraut.

OLD-FASHIONED SAUERKRAUT

2 cups shredded organic white cabbage

⅓ cup whey (see above)

1 tablespoon pink Himalayan salt or Celtic sea salt

a little filtered water, to top up if needed

Add the cabbage to your bowl of whey. Squeeze it thoroughly into the whey with your very clean (not at all soapy) hands.

Add the salt and continue to wring, squeeze and pulse the cabbage. Once it has softened and is starting to release its liquid, push it into a jar and pour the liquid over the top of it. Press it down so that it is submerged slightly and there are no air pockets in the cabbage.

Put the lid on the jar and leave it out at room temperature for 2–3 weeks, at which point it will be ready to eat. Store it in the fridge indefinitely as the flavours will just deepen over time.

IT IS IMPORTANT TO USE ORGANIC INGREDIENTS FOR THIS RECIPE AS PESTICIDES AND DETERGENTS USED TO WASH CONVENTIONAL VEGETABLES CAN INTERFERE WITH THE FERMENTATION PROCESS.

VEGETARIAN

ANTICIPATE HUNGER LIKE A NINJA

ZOE

I love my food. I have always been a planner too. I like to know at breakfast what we are having for dinner. It used to drive Damon bonkers. 'We're still eating breakfast, I don't know what I feel like for dinner,' he'd say, quite understandably. Still it didn't stop me from daydreaming, planning and concocting my next meal for days or sometimes weeks in advance.

When we had friends over for a meal, I'd spend days pottering around farmers' markets and reading recipe books, coming up with ideas for a menu, a smorgasbord of delights. It was a hobby and a passion. Now with a little one running around at my feet, I'm lucky if I get a minute to scan the fridge before I throw a few ingredients in a pan and hope they'll turn out somewhat tasty!

When life gets busy, planning and forethought often go out the window. That's why it's good to make it a habit to anticipate mealtimes and hunger before they strike. Like a ninja would his nemesis. Yeah.

While we were writing this book, Damon actually said to me, 'You have to put in the bit about how I get grumpy when I forget to eat and then I want to eat chocolate.'

I said, 'I was going to mention it but I didn't want to throw you under the bus.'

'Throw me under the bus,' he replied. Bless him. So here goes.

Damon forgets to eat. Not just occasionally, but almost daily when he's busy. He gets so wound up in what he's doing that he simply forgets. He won't even notice he's hungry until he's starving. It hits him suddenly: he'll be wondering why he's tired and narky, then I'll ask him if he's eaten yet . . . and he'll reply that he hasn't. I'm sure low-blood sugar is responsible for most of life's futile 'I don't even know what we are fighting about' disagreements.

I'm at the opposite end of the spectrum, like I said – planning meals well in advance. I might forget other things, like when the bins go out or when the car registration is due but food isn't one of them. As soon as my stomach hints at a rumble, I'm thinking about food. I go to the kitchen and start preparing a meal, which can take anywhere from 5 minutes to half an hour if I'm feeling fancy, and by the time I've finished making it I'm certainly hungry and ready to eat.

I've learnt with Damon that I need to anticipate his hunger and just make us both lunch, knowing that he'll eat it even if right now he's

'If you can be regular and consistent with mealtimes, you're less likely to make rash and unhealthy decisions.'

not aware of his desire for it. I've learnt the hard way what happens if I don't. He just eats *my* lunch and I end up making more. (You can guess who is hungry and grumpy now, right?)

And I'm happy to say he's getting better at knowing he needs to anticipate his own hunger. Still, when he's working he often forgets and this usually means he makes more rushed and poor choices food-wise, which inevitably affects his mood.

I know many parents who can relate to this behaviour in their children and who will certainly notice the effects on a teenager's mood if they walk through the door at afternoon tea time and there is nothing in the fridge (I've written more about kids and sugar on page 138).

If you are like Damon, you will need to start practising eating regularly. Snacking is better than forgetting entirely because at least you'll be getting something nourishing in and avoiding the crash and mood changes that can come with skipping meals. If you can be regular and consistent and kind to your body with mealtimes, you're less likely to make rash and unhealthy decisions that create a cycle of dependency.

ZOE'

121

SUGAR *and* ALCOHOL

This subject gets the Q&A Grand Prize. This was the topic raised at every single one of the Q&As throughout Australia and New Zealand. Although the question was often dressed up as 'How much sugar is in alcohol?', the subtext always screamed, 'Please tell me I can still drink! I can lose the apple juice or the Just Right, but f#%k you, sugarman, if I can't have a beer or a wine!'

Well, the good news is that of course you can still have a drink. We need to be kind to ourselves with this new approach to sugar. Sometimes people want to go to extremes and cut out everything straight away but, although that may work for some, it isn't necessary for everyone.

The news with booze is that in order to make alcohol, you need to ferment sugar and quite often that sugar is fructose, the one we are looking to avoid. (You would need to drink a lot more alcohol to get the same results I did from drinking sports drinks, juices and vitamin waters, however.)

Even though much of the fructose is burnt off in the fermentation process, it's important to remember that excess alcohol does have other metabolic effects on your body. It gets processed by the liver and given we now know the important role this organ plays (see page 10), I would recommend keeping the drinking to a minimum while doing the sugar transition. Let the liver heal itself from all the years of sugar abuse first so it can start to do its job properly. Remember the 'liver lying in a hospital bed' metaphor? Well, the last thing it needs is someone constantly pouring scotch or wine on its head while it's trying to recover.

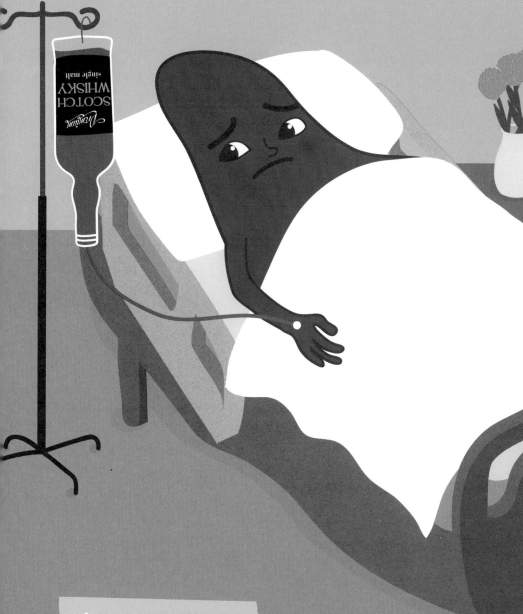

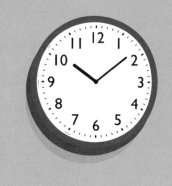

^ LET YOUR LIVER HEAL PROPERLY

the BOOZE TEASPOON COUNT

Here's a handy (or bloody annoying) guide explaining the sugar content of some popular social lubricants.

Please note: these amounts vary slightly depending on the brand.

CHAMPAGNE:

½– 2 teaspoons

WHITE WINE:

⅓ teaspoon

RED WINE:

⅕ teaspoon

DESSERT WINE:

5–8 teaspoons

DESSERT WINES *are often very high in sugar. Sugar or grape concentrate is often added after the fermentation process to add sweetness. (This is known as chaptilisation in case you ever need it at a trivia night.)*

LONG ISLAND ICED TEA:

9 teaspoons

MIKE'S HARD LEMONADE:

8 teaspoons

PRE-MIXED DRINKS:
Very high sugar; some like Rockstar Vodka flavours have 14 teaspoons.

BACARDI BREEZER TYPE DRINKS:
Just look at the colour – very high in sugar. Consider them boozy desserts.

WHISKEY, VODKA, RUM, GIN:
All these are made by fermenting sugar or grains and contain no added sugar. It's only when you add mixers that the sugar content skyrockets. (cheeky tonic water)

VODKA AND SODA:

0 teaspoons.

VODKA AND TONIC:

(350 ml) 7 teaspoons

GIN AND TONIC:

(350 ml) 7 teaspoons

VODKA AND CRANBERRY:

12 teaspoons

MOJITO:

5 teaspoons

BAILEYS:

12 teaspoons

WHISKEY SOUR:

5 teaspoons

PORT:

5 teaspoons

MARGARITA:

8 teaspoons

FROZEN MARGARITA:

14½ teaspoons

CIDER:

3–7 teaspoons

BEER: *Contains a sugar called maltose, which is not as dangerous as fructose but is still high in glucose molecules, so terrific at spiking that insulin and storing fat.*

WHAT DO I EAT IF I'M OUT?

This was another very high-ranking question from the Q&A patrons: How do you go with sugar when you're eating out?

Well, despite spending nearly four years breathing in nothing but the topic of sugar (and the occasional nappy aroma), Zoe and I are surprisingly lax when it comes to eating out. I am not saying that we regularly share a jug of Fanta or ask for BBQ sauce on our creme brulee; more that we aren't inclined to badger waiters and insist on knowing how many teaspoons of sugar are in the sauce.

We have an understanding that as long as we are diligent at home, then every now and then when we come across sugar in our dining travels, that's okay. There are still ways to be smart about it, though. Here are some things to be aware of when you are out at a restaurant and relying on others to do the cooking (and the dishes) for you:

KEY THOUGHT: ALWAYS THINK GRILLED, ROASTED OR STEAMED RATHER THAN FRIED.

* **Avoid the sauces**: As you are probably aware by now, sugar and sauces have a passionate love affair going on. They struggle to live without each other and when they are together it's like a newly-in-lust teenage couple groping in public. Ask for the sauce on the side so you can apply it at your own discretion or place the pashing lovebirds on the other side of the table behind the napkins and out of sight.

* **Avoid the refined carbs and fried starches**: This becomes much easier when you get into a groove. I now look for things on the menu that have a good dose of protein, healthy fats and vegetables. If you just have to have a chicken parma, order it with salad and no fries. Choose the fish or steak with veggies, go easy on the pasta with creamy sauce, and try to resist the basket of white bread in the centre of the table, no matter how peckish you are.

* **Always choose water:** Don't be drawn into a soft drink or juice with your meal. Go for fizzy water with a slice of lemon if you feel like really letting your hair down. Of course there may be alcohol involved, but make sure that's your only beverage indulgence. Resist the alcohol-and-soft-drink liquid calorie tsunami. Nobody comes out alive.

SUGAR AND SAUCES ARE LIKE A NEWLY-IN-LUST TEENAGE COUPLE GROPING IN PUBLIC.

- **Think ahead:** If you know you are heading out to dinner with friends and are going to indulge and have a fun night, then perhaps keep your sugar eating at the start of the day to a minimum. Remember the WHO recommends no more than 6 teaspoons a day for optimal health, so don't blow that amount on a glass of apple juice or low-fat yoghurt in the morning when you can cover yourself in sticky date pudding after dark.

- **Think ahead again:** Try not to go out on a totally empty stomach or you may be lured into the 'bread trap'. This rears its head in that pre-ordering, chatting, casual-drink phase of dining. You aren't really conscious of eating because you're too busy catching up on the goss and before you know it you've downed half a loaf of white bread or half a dozen bread sticks. Eating high-fibre foods half an hour before heading out will help you step around the bread trap. Try almonds, a pear and cheese, or a carrot (see page 112 for more high-fibre options).

- **Kids' menu:** Don't fall into the trap of ordering from the kids' menu just because it's there. Invariably it is a cue for the chef to kick-start the deep-fryer and roll out the refined carbs. Instead order something from the main menu with protein, veggies and healthy fats, but just in a smaller portion.

- **Dessert:** Zoe and I are not big dessert people any more but we often just ask for some berries and fresh cream. Remember, if your sugar intake is low then some delicious saturated fat with mini fructose bursts encased in protective fibre ain't gonna hurt. If you do need to smash a creme brulee or the sticky date then sharing with others is a good idea. Three spoons, please? (Not giant 1970s salad serving spoons though – that's clearly cheating.)

When you are happy with your health you may occasionally hoover down a pad Thai or destroy a few slices of Hawaiian pizza. The key message is to just move away from making these types of food a regular part of your eating experience. Let them be a very occasional treat. The beautiful irony is that you may not actually enjoy them when you do go back. You are likely to be far more sensitive to these types of foods once you have switched your fuel supply to the more efficient variety. I hear this all the time and it's a sure sign of being on the right track.

Which Cuisine?

Sushi is okay but sashimi is better. Go easy on the rice, especially if you are easing off a high-sugar diet.

Indian food loves sugar in its sauces, but the amount can vary from region to region. Some dishes use raisins or dates as the sweetener. The main culprits to avoid during the transition are the tempting naans and lots of rice. (By the way, my best friend, who has Indian heritage, dreams of opening an award-winning Indian restaurant called 'Second to Naan'.)

Making the film I learnt the sad truth about why I love Thai food so much. It's full of sugar. My dear, dear friend Pad Thai has around 7 teaspoons in a small serve and 14 in a large. Imagine pouring a can of Red Bull over 2-minute noodles and then adding bean sprouts. Zoe has made her own version on page 74, but as much as I love her cooking, I will still have the occasional reunion with my old friend. The soups and broths are, however, the better option.

It's not great news when it comes to Chinese food either. As a child, I loved sweet and sour pork, honey chicken and lemon chicken. *So* much sugar – pretty much the scene from the film where I ate sugar poured over chicken. I recently saw a recipe for orange chicken that had more sugar in it than a triple chocolate thickshake from McDonalds. Choose wisely: avoid sauces and go for the green vegetables.

Pizza, the traditional way, is really a no-go during the transition, unless you want to make them at home and use our special base (see page 169 for the recipe).

If you're at the local cafe for lunch, try to resist sandwiches. Choose the fillings but have them with salad and egg, avocado, vegetables or cheese instead. You may return to wholegrain bread down the track but for now give it a miss (see page 49 for my take on grains). Watch the dressing, condiments or packaged mayonnaise too – remember the groping teenagers?.

Now there may come a day when the kids are screaming in the back seat, you're running late and you just have to pull the car into a fast-food joint of some description. I have been there myself. All I can say is: just choose water with the meal. Get the burger or chicken wrap thingy if you must, but *please* don't get the soft drink or juice. Use water to wash down the chemicals and sugar and weird oils.

ZOE

HOW TO HELP THOSE YOU LOVE
WITHOUT BEING A NAG

It's always tempting when we discover something new that works for us, such as reducing sugar intake, to tell anyone and everyone who will listen. This is fine as long as they are interested. However, sometimes we have a friend or loved one who is not only *not* interested, but actually resistant. Obviously we have gained enough positive changes from our own experience that warrant us telling them in the first place; we care about them and hope they too can feel as good as we do. This is where it can come unstuck. You see, change has to come internally. It has to come from our friend or partner's own willing-ness and in their own time.

So here are a few tips for these sorts of situations and an example of how I have applied them in my own life. I hope they help you navigate a time of transition and stay true to your new ways while remaining understand-ing of others' choices along the way.

* Walk your talk
Rather than trying to 'convert' everyone in your life to cut down on sugar, just do it yourself and let them to witness the changes through your example. They might notice enough to be curious, and then once they are open they can decide for themselves if it suits their lifestyle.

* Allow for differences of opinion while standing your ground
Sometimes we encounter a particularly opposing viewpoint to our own and when this happens it can be tempting to become righteous. Rather than going down this path, try to understand the other person's view. The more we push against it, the more stubborn they can sometimes become. Stay true to your own discoveries if they work for you and again demonstrate through your actions what works.

A little example from my own life:

I remember going away with a group of friends some years ago. Back then I had made choices about my health and wellbeing that meant I was eating and drinking differently to everyone else there. One such difference was that I drank coconuts while they all drank wine! I think they all thought I was a bit coco-nuts at the time. (I know someone out there is saying to themselves, 'Coconuts contain fructose!' but hey, a girl's gotta party sometimes, right?) Instead of insisting they 'be like me', I just carried on with what I found worked and let them enjoy their drunkenness and the hangovers! Six years later and a few kids between us all, some of the group have studied nutrition and others have also made positive changes around their health, and now out of these friends I would say 80 per cent are not only drinking coconuts, but some are fermenting them as well! The point is, I didn't force them. They all made these choices in their own time and in their own way. Perhaps the way I helped is that when they did, I was an anchor point they could relate to while making their own transitions.

* Offer to be the chef

This worked particularly well for me. If you're the one who does most of the cooking in the house, start making low-sugar meals that are so delicious everyone enjoys them and no one notices the changes being made for them. They might start to feel different and then become curious as to why, at which point you might be able to explain some of the finer details and be received with greater interest.

A final point: If someone is actively deriding your choice to change your diet, then understand this usually comes from their own insecurity at losing the 'you' they are currently familiar with. You can reassure them that you still love them and carry on anyway. Be true to you. Remember that at some point you made the decision to reduce sugar consumption and make conscious choices about your health from an informed place (possibly from witnessing Damon's journey in the film). Trust that others will do the same in their own time if it is for them. Otherwise, let them be. Good luck and remember lots of people are in the same boat – you aren't alone.

Zoe

SNACKING

Given that the current food environment really isn't set up to kindly nurture people through a low-sugar life, it pays to plan ahead when you are going to leave the sanctuary of your own home.

Your best weapon against the sugary neon-advertising blitzkrieg is a constant blood-sugar level. If those levels plummet when you are out, you will be drawn to a convenience store like a mosquito to a blue buzzing light. You'll just want the immediate pretend satiety of a refined carbohydrate and although it may take years longer than the sudden, fiery implosion of the mosquito, the end result could be the same.

I always try to take something to snack on when driving into town or on the train. A handful of nuts will do, or some fruit with a hunk of cheese. You just want to keep your engine purring away nicely in between meals like an accomplished, seasoned driver. You don't want to drop the revs and then seek out something to get them back up quickly again like an 'L' plater bunny-hopping around a car park. (That was my final human body/car metaphor. Thank you.)

Here are some snack swap ideas to help you through the day:

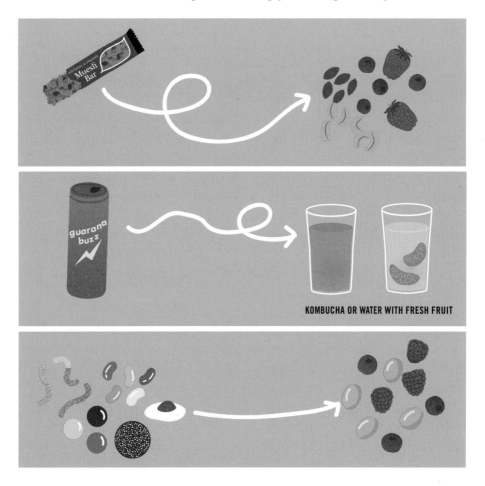

KOMBUCHA OR WATER WITH FRESH FRUIT

SWEET TREATS

Last Easter was a really interesting time for me. It was the first Festival of Cocoa since the film's release and, as you can imagine, it pushed up a lot of emotion and confusion for some people. *That Sugar Film* Facebook page alerts lit up like a switchboard after a news anchor has dropped the f-bomb on the national news.

It made me think about Easter and the chocolate-gorging festival it has become. In a world without hidden sugar everywhere, it's a nice principle: we have one day a year where we come together with family and thoroughly enjoy and indulge in some treats.

Unfortunately Easter has turned into a marketing cash cow for the confectionary industry and we now bury our children in a dazzling array of chocolate rabbits and eggs, and sugar-laced *Frozen* merchandise. The issue, of course, is that many of us are now eating the equivalent of three chocolate rabbits' worth of sugar hidden in other foods every day of the year.

If you are going to lower your sugar intake and be more conscious about how much you are actually consuming, then you will be able to have the occasional treat. There will be exceptions (like me) who are just too sensitive to added sugar so are better off avoiding it all together. Us delicate folk will enjoy the sweet recipes on pages 218–227 because they predominantly use fruit as the sweetener and don't have the overwhelming 'refined' taste that many processed sugars do.

It's important to understand that if you aren't overly sensitive to sugar, then you can still enjoy it. As we now know, the World Health Squad advises up to 6 teaspoons a day for optimal health, so some coconut sugar, maple syrup or honey in a treat isn't going to cause any major damage (as long as it doesn't make you crave more the next day, like it does with me).

When it comes to sugar alternatives, remember that most contain relatively high amounts of fructose, which is what we are trying to ease back on. Sure, coconut sugar may have a tiny bit of inulin (fibre) compared to refined sugar, and maple syrup or honey may have some antioxidants and minerals, but they are all very similar at a molecular level and so should be put in the 'treats' category (table sugar is 50 per cent fructose, high fructose corn syrup 55 per cent, honey 40 per cent, maple syrup 40 per cent, coconut sugar 40 per cent, and agave 90 per cent). This goes for rice malt syrup too. It doesn't contain fructose but is still regarded as an 'added sugar' by the World Heath Smarty Pants Club and due to it being pure glucose, it will affect your insulin, so throw it into the 'occasional treats' basket.

'If you aren't overly sensitive to sugar, then you can still enjoy it.'

Zoe and I often talk about this topic with regards to our own daughter. Our plan is to give her our homemade sugar-free treats. We hope this will 'define' her palate and so if she tastes the refined version it will be too sweet or overbearing. This worked with Zoe, who cannot go near processed sugars now. But please check back in in four years when our daughter has well and truly hit the children's birthday party circuit. I may well be practising the 'art of surrender' on a daily basis and laughing at the naivety of what I have just written.

ZOE

I use a variety of ingredients as 'sweet substitutes' in my recipes. My key sweeteners are fruit, including bananas, berries and dates (used sparingly and only occasionally), coconut cream and hazelnuts, as well as herbs and spices such as vanilla, cinnamon, licorice and mint. Once your palate has adjusted (see page 14), you'll notice how sweet carrots can be too.

As a rule of thumb, when I use fruit as a sweetener I include no more than I would eat on its own in one sitting. For example, in the Summer Salad on page 176, I include three nectarines for 4 serves, which equates to about 3 pieces of nectarine each. In the smoothies on pages 162–63, I use 1 banana for 2 serves.

When you use whole foods in their natural form or as close to their natural form as possible, you will experience the difference for yourself. Maybe even do a little test and after a couple of months of using this guide, try a mouthful of something sweet that you previously ate regularly and see if you can notice the difference. It will probably taste saccharine and leave a slightly unpleasant taste in your mouth. You may feel a little 'buzzy' or even headachy, which is what can happen to me after I have processed fruit juice. This is a sign you're doing well!

ZOE

POLITE SUGAR

Zoe

So your dear parents have invited you around for a special meal to celebrate your Great Aunty Thelma's hundredth birthday. She can hardly hear you when you wish her happy birthday. 'What?' she asks. You lean in to repeat it closer to her hearing aid: 'Happy bir—', but she cuts you off mid-sentence by landing a big swalk on your kisser and says, 'Have some cake, love.' Her shaky, arthritic fingers clutch at a plate of triple-whipped pavlova dripping with jammy sauce, cream and kiwi fruit. Do you take the plate?

Call me old-fashioned but OF COURSE YOU DO! Whether or not you actually then eat it is up to you, though. I would probably just pass it along to Damon as I'm not really a pavlova fan. If it were chocolate cake, however, I'd politely and delightedly polish it off!

I call this social conundrum 'polite sugar'. (Maybe this can be another hashtag along with #paladjustment. If you find yourself in a sticky situation, unsure of whether or not to have a #politesugar moment, take a photo and launch it into the social sphere and see what response you get!

In some social situations it's more important to respect the feelings of another than to be rigid in your thinking. However, 'polite sugar' is not to be confused with repeatedly compromising your values or finding a convenient excuse to do so. If you are lucky enough to see Great Aunty Thelma every week and she pushes the cake on you, you can absolutely decline. It's no longer 'polite sugar' if you see her all the time – it's just sugar.

#politesugar

FEEDING YOUR FAMILY

This next section is about how to offer your child new food choices while still allowing them the freedom to form their own opinions. Children are savvy. I remember very well being 15 or 16 and knowing I knew a lot more than my parents already (although I know now how little I actually knew!). But the point is, when we were children or young adults, the environment around food was rather different from what it is now. I don't remember being bombarded by the same level of advertising, for example.

You can't deny children sweet things while consuming them yourself. They will want what you want and want what you have. Already I see it with our own baby girl. When we are out at a cafe and I order a tea, she wants one as well. Enter the babycino (sans marshmallows, of course), which I always thought was a bit of a wank until I understood little children want to be like us big people. It seems inbuilt and primal: 'If they can have it, then I want it too!' or 'If it's good enough for them, it's good enough for me!'

If your child is currently eating large amounts of sugar and is reluctant to change their ways, the bottom line is that as the adult you probably created or were party to creating the situation in the first place. Children do as we do, not as we say. We need to recognise our own contributions to our children's behaviour and start to 'unplug' any areas that no longer fit within the lifestyle we want to create.

'Make your home a haven.'

The first step is to make your home a haven. Empty your cupboards of anything you no longer wish your family to consume. You can do this overtly if you have full family support or more gently, by explaining that once the current cereal box, block of chocolate or biscuit tin is finished, you will not be restocking it.

The second step is crucial to the longevity of your family's change. You must offer nourishing and delicious alternatives to the old favourites that are being replaced. This may mean eating at home more often, being regular with mealtimes and making sure you are a step ahead of any hungry teenagers that might be about to burst through the door insisting on a bowl of Fruit Loops for afternoon tea!

Anticipate your family's needs (like a ninja – see page 120) and give them plenty of hearty alternatives before the hunger strikes or you may just have a hunger strike on your hands!

During this transition, it's important to explain and be patient. Children are usually quick and willing to change if you give them a proper explanation. They mostly want their parents' approval and love as much

'Explain and be patient.'

as we want theirs. Offer them a clear and concise explanation about why you are changing what's on the menu and stick to it. Try to be positive in your explanation rather than negative. For example: 'We are changing the way we eat because we will all have more energy and feel better' or 'We are just trying something new for a change. Let's see how we all find it for while'. Please avoid hurtful and negative statements, which can create upset, such as: 'Because you go crazy when you eat sugar.' (This is an intentionally mild example but you get the drift.)

It is also unnecessary and potentially harmful to comment on body shape or size. This is a tender topic for adults, let alone developing children. Only broach it if it is initiated or actively invited by your child and even then be very gentle. The focus here is on how a change in diet makes us *feel*. Any other effects are a by-product and ideally shouldn't be made the sole focus. And of course for further advice, refer to an expert.

Once you've explained what's happening, you then need to take a deep breath, or perhaps many deep breaths, and be patient. Your family may take a while to embrace a new way of eating, especially if they were used to a lot of sugar before. The bridging week recipes are here to help with this transition (see pages 56–95). If you have a 'three-ager' you might hear 'But why?' a thousand times or more before they start to enjoy their veggie sticks! Alternatively, you may be surprised by how easy the transition can be for everyone. In fact some children may welcome it immediately, as they often often seem to have an innate radar for ideas that bring more harmony, love and joy into their lives, wise beings that they are.

HELPING YOUR CHILD
TO DEVELOP HEALTHY HABITS

Here are more ways to encourage and assist your child in developing healthy taste preferences and habits.

* Remember, babies don't know what refined sugar is yet, so why not make fruit out to be the most wonderful sweet treat there is? This may even influence their palates, which means the refined stuff will taste too strong as they get older. And remember there is actually no biological requirement for 'added sugar' in our diet – we can get all the fructose or glucose we need from natural sources.

* Our daughter just wants to mimic what we do. All she knows is blueberries or frozen mango as a sweet snack and loves them, just as we do. I will make my own dark chocolate or we will buy some fancy bitter variety every now and then, but when we do, we are open to giving our daughter a try. The last thing we want to do is to give her a complex about it.

* Some supermarkets offer free fruit for kids when they go shopping with their parents. What a great way to enjoy 'nature's dessert'.

* Now admittedly we haven't hit the 'kids' sugar party circuit' yet but I take great comfort from David Gillespie and what he has experienced. He has six children so has seen it all! He provides a clean house free of sugar, and when his children go to parties they occasionally indulge but not as much as the other kids. This is because he describes them as almost being 'hung over' the next day. Because they don't have the sugary treats very often, their tolerance is low and so it really affects them. This means they don't go quite as hard the next time around.

* Language is important. We try not to use the word 'treat' around Velvet: we prefer 'once in a while' food. The notion of a treat sets up an emotional response and a reward, and even glorifies the food. If you make the 'treat' too special, then the demand for it will only increase.

PARTIES, SLEEPOVERS AND OTHER SUGAR DENS

My 12th birthday party was at the local ice rink and I had a huge slice of black forest cake, probably followed by a squillion sour worms and topped off with a couple of chilli warheads, which were a big thing at the time. Point is, I'm still standing. Not only that, I'm writing a book about how to reduce sugar intake. So you can relax, parents. Every now and then situations will get out of hand and that's kind of okay. It's how we learn.

It's when there is a birthday party every weekend, followed by a sports day, and a local fete and then the Easter show with a thousand lolly bags, that the balance becomes out of whack and we need to start ramping up the awareness.

A lot of the time, your child's consumption of highly processed sugary food at these events is as much about fitting in with friends as anything else. There will be occasions when you may need to pull in the reins and create terms that you and your child both agree upon to bring some structure to the situation.

For example:

'You have a sleepover party tomorrow night and your school fair is coming up, so can we agree that you only have sweet lollies or chips at one of those and a proper lunch at the other?'

Be realistic, firm and fair. Decide on the terms together and then trust your child to follow through. You might offer one gentle reminder at most, ideally none.

If your child does break your agreement, be honest and show your disappointment but there is no need to drum it in. Their own conscience will tell them what is right and what isn't. They won't feel good about letting you down and in future will probably try harder to make a different choice.

Above all, remember that your children are discovering the world for themselves. Let them. Being a healthy, kind, loving example is the best thing you can do.

HEALTHY LUNCHBOXES

Lunch at school is an important meal and it's also probably one of the times parents feel least in control about their child's choices. Kids are often heavily influenced by the need to fit in with their friends. That said, they are also very savvy and flexible and often willing to make changes when they understand why they are happening.

If your child has been used to a certain lunch, then try modifying it gradually. You can dilute juice down little by little or perhaps switch sandwich bread for a wrap variety that's a little more wholegrain. Earmark recipes that they like and make them a staple in your kitchen. If there is a meal they particularly enjoy at dinner, offer it to them again as a lunch leftover the following day.

Flavoured yoghurts are a popular snack, but they are often heavily sugar-laden. Replace them with unsweetened plain yoghurt with real fruit added (see page 35 for ideas).

Get your kids involved if they are willing or just gradually and discreetly make the changes yourself if they are not. Either way, tread gently and be fair.

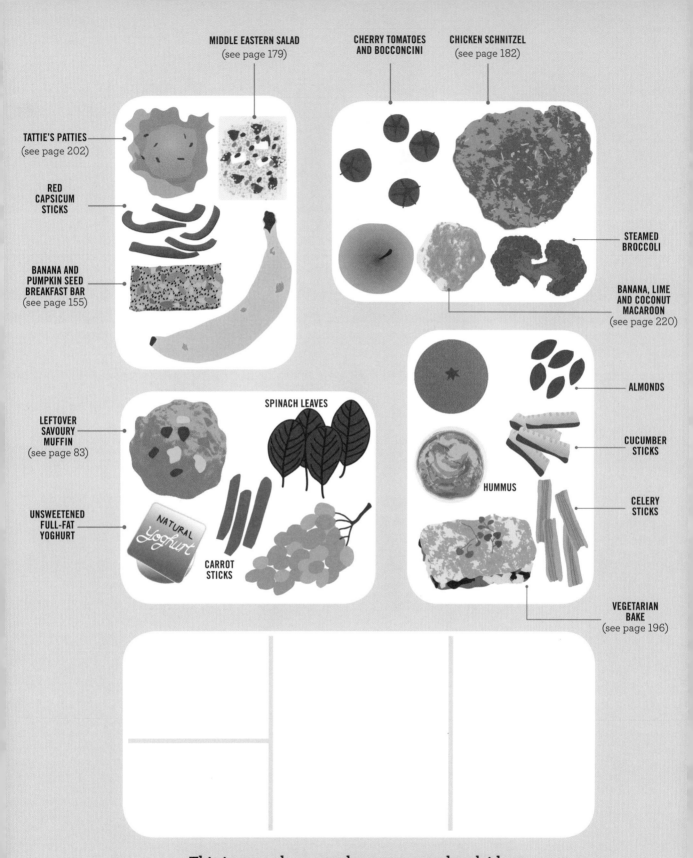

MIDDLE EASTERN SALAD
(see page 179)

CHERRY TOMATOES
AND BOCCONCINI

CHICKEN SCHNITZEL
(see page 182)

TATTIE'S PATTIES
(see page 202)

RED
CAPSICUM
STICKS

STEAMED
BROCCOLI

BANANA AND
PUMPKIN SEED
BREAKFAST BAR
(see page 155)

BANANA, LIME
AND COCONUT
MACAROON
(see page 220)

ALMONDS

LEFTOVER
SAVOURY
MUFFIN
(see page 83)

SPINACH LEAVES

CUCUMBER
STICKS

HUMMUS

CELERY
STICKS

UNSWEETENED
FULL-FAT
YOGHURT

NATURAL
Yoghurt

CARROT
STICKS

VEGETARIAN
BAKE
(see page 196)

This is your chance to draw your own lunch ideas.
Please take a photo and upload to #realfoodrecipes

143

TIPS FOR BABIES AND TODDLERS

Conventional supermarket toddler foods often contain high amounts of fruit juice concentrate (added sugar). Here are some ideas based on my own experiences cooking for our baby girl, Velvet.

Keep it simple: cook one meal with elements that feed the whole family: look out for recipes marked baby-friendly and toddler-friendly throughout this book. Make vegetable soups all the family can share (my pumpkin soup recipe from *That Sugar Book* is the easiest thing in the world to make and is purely pumpkin). I also pureeed various combinations of the food we were having to put in reusable sucky pouches. I prefer these to containers as they were just less messy and easier for Velvet to use, plus she could eat them on the go. The pouches also store and freeze well so you can make a big batch of your baby's favourite meal and save it for later.

In the early stages of introducing solids, adding a little breastmilk to new food is enough to sweeten and make it 'familiar' to bubs.

Once her teeth were well established and chewing was getting easier, we offered almost everything to Velvet, usually cut up into small pieces or sometimes offered whole so she could tear it apart with her new fangs. I occasionally peeled fruit such as apples to make it easier to manage, though now she's bigger she manages them whole very nicely.

Offer variety. Some of our daughter's early favourites included avocado, broccoli, green beans, bone marrow and lamb chops (to suck on). She even quite liked small amounts of chilli and lemon. Another unusual and very gourmet early favourite was fish roe (aka caviar), which she tried at a party at her grandma's house and couldn't get enough of – much to the trepidation of Daddy as he clutched at his wallet! A lot of the time babies are experimenting with texture as much as anything, so offer them this variety of experience they are seeking.

Whatever food we gave our baby, we were right there supervising making sure she was safe from potential choking hazards, especially pre-tooth! (Cherry tomatoes and grapes I'm looking at you – cutting them in half usually does the trick.) A close nurse friend of mine once reassured me that little babies do have a good gag reflex though and usually anything too uncomfortable for them just comes back out.

Of course, there will be occasions when you are caught off-guard at meal times with a toddler. If you do opt for supermarket quick fixes, stick to vegetable-based purees, which contain a tiny amount of fruit, and avoid the predominantly fruit-based ones.

the
CONSOLIDATION
PHASE
RECIPES

QUINOA PORRIDGE

SERVES 3–4

1 cup white quinoa

1 cup raw unsalted cashews

1 cup full-fat coconut milk

1 tablespoon ground cinnamon plus extra, to sprinkle

1 teaspoon vanilla extract

berries, sliced banana or Chia Jam (see page 160), to serve

My dear friend Marcia inspired this recipe. One cold winter's morning, after a sleepover at hers, she made a raspberry version of this for me when I had to be at work by 5 am! She even gave me some to enjoy later, and I can vouch that it's as delicious cold as it is warm. It is almost like a rice pudding. If you're craving something substantial that will keep you going and in the past would have eaten something like oatmeal, you'll find this a welcome substitute.

I recommend making a batch of quinoa and freezing it to have on hand to add to salads, etc., instead of consuming other, more refined, carbs. The cooking technique here is the perfect way to make quinoa without burning it.

Place the quinoa and 1 cup of water in a small saucepan and bring to the boil. Pop the lid on and reduce the heat to a simmer. Cook for 15 minutes until the water has been absorbed, then turn off the heat and fluff up the quinoa with a fork. Put the lid back on and leave to rest for 5 minutes.

Add the cashews, coconut milk, cinnamon, vanilla and ½ cup of water to the pan. Simmer over medium–low heat for about 10 minutes until the quinoa is plump and the cashews have softened.

Serve warm with berries or banana on top and a sprinkling of cinnamon. It's also good with a scoop of chia jam.

> NOTE FROM DAMON:
> FOR THOSE BALKING AT
> THE SIGHT OF 'GRAINS',
> PLEASE SEE PAGE 49! THIS
> IS A BREAKFAST FOR ACTIVE,
> GROWING CHILDREN,
> AND ADULTS TOO.

VEGAN   LEFTOVERS   TODDLER FRIENDLY

BAKED BREAKFAST RICOTTA

MAKES 6

butter, for greasing and frying

4 bacon rashers, chopped

100 g mushrooms, roughly chopped

250 g fresh ricotta, drained

2 free-range eggs

1 tablespoon thyme leaves

When you need a substantial breakfast to carry you through a busy morning, these will do the trick. If there are any leftovers, they are great for the lunchbox too.

· ·

Preheat the oven to 180°C. Grease a 6-hole muffin tray and set aside.

In a large frying pan, melt a small nub of butter and fry the bacon and mushroom together for a few minutes, stirring all the while.

Meanwhile, in a mixing bowl, whisk together the ricotta and eggs. Evenly divide the ricotta mixture among the muffin holes until they are half-full.

Stir the thyme into the mushroom and bacon, then remove the pan from the heat. Divide the bacon mix among the muffin holes, gently pressing it into the ricotta with a fork as you go to loosely combine the layers.

Pop them in the oven and bake for about 20 minutes or until puffed up.

NOTE FROM DAMON:
WHEN YOU CUT BACK ON SUGAR AND REFINED CARBOHYDRATES, RICOTTA BECOMES A VERY GOOD FRIEND AND ADDS A WONDERFUL FLAVOUR AND SUBSTANCE.

LEFTOVERS

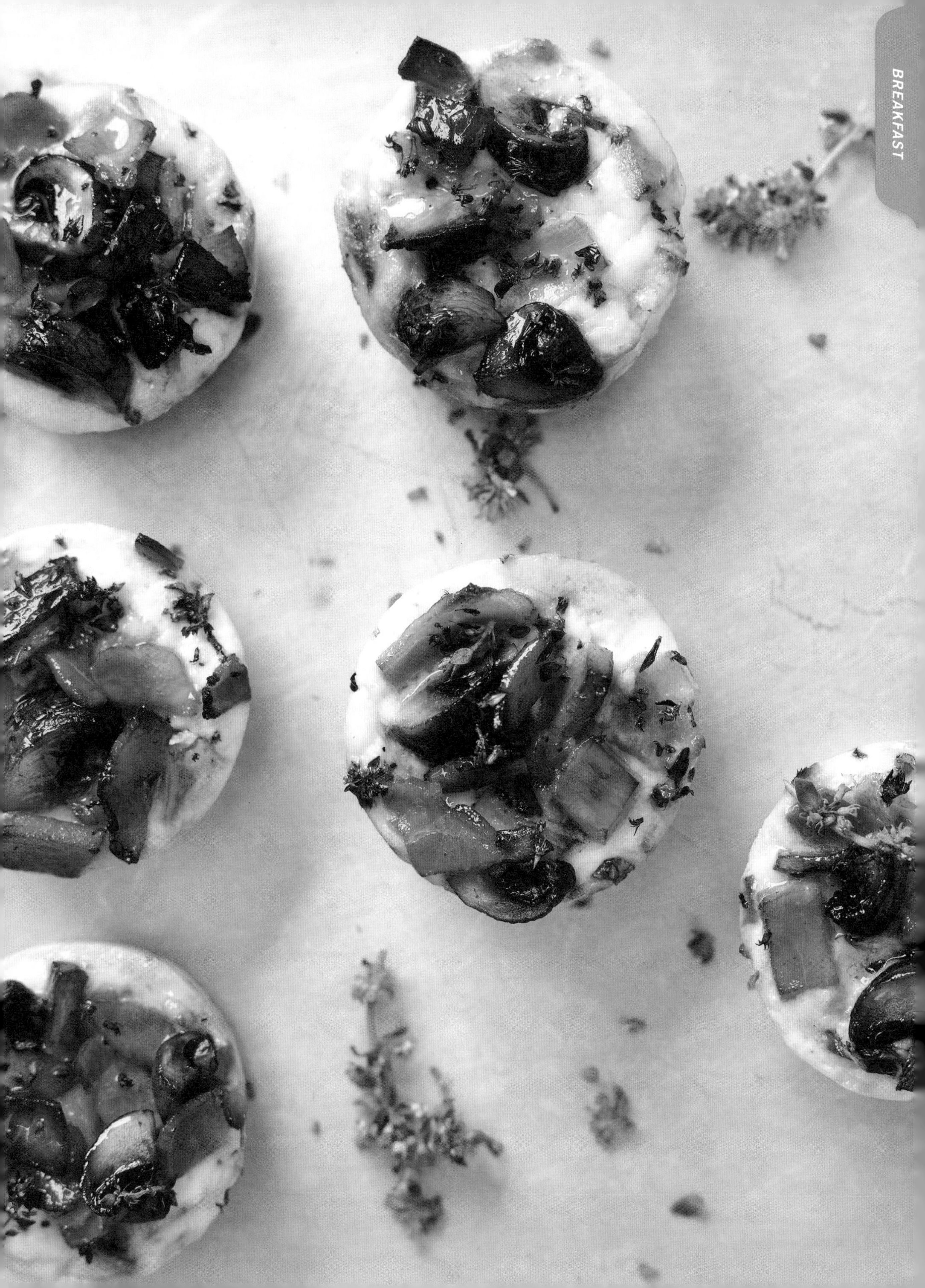

COCONUT PIKELETS *with* BUTTER-BERRY SAUCE

SERVES 4

BUTTER-BERRY SAUCE

1 tablespoon butter

3 cups blueberries, chopped strawberries or raspberries (or a combination of all three)

1 teaspoon vanilla extract

¾ cup coconut oil, melted

COCONUT PIKELETS

4 free-range eggs (preferably at room temperature)

1½ cups full-fat coconut milk

½ teaspoon bicarbonate of soda

⅔ cup fine coconut flour

butter, for frying

NOTE FROM DAMON:
OBVIOUSLY THIS ISN'T AN EVERYDAY BREAKFAST – BUT IT IS A GREAT WAY TO KICKSTART A VERY CASUAL SUNDAY.

There are many variations of this recipe floating around at the moment. I've made sure this version is as simple and affordable as possible, while remaining wonderfully tasty and close to the more traditional recipe.

• •

To make the butter-berry sauce, melt the butter in a small saucepan over medium–low heat. Add the berries and vanilla, crushing the berries gently with a fork for a minute while they soften. Cover with the coconut oil, then turn the heat down to very low and let the berries gently warm and fizz in the oil for a couple of minutes. Remove the pan from the heat and set aside while you make the pancakes.

For the pikelets, whisk the eggs until they are frothy, then gradually pour in the coconut milk and continue to whisk. Add the bicarb of soda and then the coconut flour and stir through until mixture is well-combined and the flour has absorbed some of the moisture of the eggs and milk.

In a large frying pan over medium heat, melt some butter and spoon out a few tablespoons of batter; one large pan should accommodate 3–4 small pikelets. You may need to spread the batter a little with the back of a spoon to even out the thickness. Pop the lid on the frying pan to steam the pikelets through a little as they cook. After a couple of minutes, gently lift up a pikelet (these are very soft, so be gentle) and flip it to check if the underside is brown. If it is, go ahead and flip the rest to brown the other side. Remove from the heat and place on some paper towel to absorb any excess butter and keep them warm by piling them up. Repeat with the remaining batter.

To serve, plate a few pikelets in a stack and spoon the warm butter-berry sauce over the top.

VEGETARIAN   TODDLER FRIENDLY

BANANA *and* PUMPKIN SEED BREAKFAST BAR

MAKES 8

½ ripe banana

½ cup sunflower seeds

½ cup pumpkin seeds

1 cup white chia seeds

1 teaspoon ground cinnamon

1 teaspoon vanilla extract

1 teaspoon salt

1 teaspoon coconut oil

Nowadays, a lot of places, including planes and schools, don't allow nut bars due to widespread allergies. This seed bar is the answer to this conundrum and is ideal for breakfast on the go. Below is a basic recipe which you can adjust by adding fruit or raw cacao powder or your own favourites to create some variation.

Preheat the oven to 120°C and line a 26 × 16 cm baking tin with baking paper.

In a large bowl, mash the banana with a fork, then stir in the remaining ingredients and mix together well. (Or you can use a food processor to combine – just use the pulse button.)

Press the mixture firmly into the prepared tin to form a 2.5-cm-thick layer. Pop in the oven for about 1 hour to slowly firm up. Make sure you check on it as it bakes and remove it when it is the consistency you desire; the mixture will harden even more if it is left uncovered in the fridge after baking.

Cut the mixture into 5 cm wide slices. Wrap the bars individually in baking paper tied with twine, if you like. These are best consumed within a week.

> NOTE FROM DAMON:
> THESE ARE ALSO SENSATIONAL SERVED WITH RICOTTA AND BANANA ON TOP.

VEGAN   LEFTOVERS

155

BREKKIE SALAD

SERVES 4

2 cups baby spinach

1 cup rocket

1 cup roughly chopped flat-leaf parsley, mint and/or basil

2 tomatoes, sliced

4 free-range eggs

salt and pepper, to taste

olive oil, for drizzling

When we are lucky enough to go out for a lazy Sunday brunch, we enjoy a version of this salad in our local cafe. It's a light, fresh option, still packed with protein.

Fill a lidded frying pan with water to a depth of about 2.5 cm deep. Bring to a simmer over medium heat.

Share the spinach and rocket out among bowls. Sprinkle the herbs and tomatoes over the top.

Turn the simmering water down to low and crack the eggs into it. Place a lid on top. After 3–5 minutes, depending on how runny you like your yolks, remove the lid and gently scoop up each egg with a slotted spoon. Let the water drain thoroughly, then gently lay an egg on top of each salad pile. Season to taste with salt and pepper and drizzle with olive oil to finish.

VEGETARIAN

SWEET POTATO *and* CORN FRITTERS

**SERVES 4
WITH LEFTOVERS**

1 large sweet potato,
halved lengthways

1 cup sweetcorn

1 free-range egg

butter, for frying

Cultured 'Cream Cheese'
(page 119), to serve

If I'm baking sweet potatoes for dinner, I like to pop an extra one in so I can make these fritters for breakfast the next day. I never usually peel sweet potatoes, as much of the fibre is in the skin (and it saves time!), but here you'll need to remove the peel to create a nice smooth texture. You can easily substitute or supplement the corn here – any half-eaten leftover fridge vegetables and herbs (I like parsley or basil) will work.

Preheat the oven to 180°C. Roast the sweet potato for 30 minutes or until soft, then leave it to cool slightly. Peel, then roughly chop it.

Place the sweet potato, corn and egg in a food processor and whizz together to combine.

Melt some butter in a frying pan over high heat. Once it sizzles, turn the heat down a little and add a heaped tablespoon of mixture to the pan, gently flattening it with a fork and shaking the pan to prevent it from sticking – you should fit about 4 fritters in the pan at a time.

Pop the lid on and let the fritters cook through for a few minutes before removing the lid and very gently flipping them to cook through for another few minutes. Remember they have no flour to bind them, so they will be softer than the usual fritters. Repeat with the remaining mixture, then use a spatula to transfer them to a serving plate. (You may wish to keep them warm in a very low oven.)

Serve the fritters warm with a scoop of 'cream cheese'.

CHIA JAM

MAKES ONE JAR

3 cups hulled, roughly chopped ripe strawberries

½ cup chia seeds

This sugar-free jam has a lovely mild flavour and is naturally more tart than commercial jam. Keep it in the fridge. This is great served with the Quinoa Porridge (page 148), Coconut Pikelets (page 152) or just stirred through plain Greek-style yoghurt.

Blend the strawberries and chia seeds together, gradually adding up to ½ cup of water as required to thin.

Pour the mixture into a small saucepan and bring to the boil over medium heat. Turn the heat down to a simmer and leave the jam to thicken up for a minute or two, stirring occasionally.

Transfer to a jar and store in the fridge.

VEGAN

SMOKED FISH SCRAMBLED EGGS

SERVES 2

4 free-range eggs

1 tablespoon pouring cream

butter, for frying

200 g smoked trout, sliced

Some fools turn their nose up at the idea of fish for breakfast. Damon was one until I served this one morning; he had no choice but to eat it beacuse he was so hungry and then – surprise surprise – he liked it. Maybe even more than a little bit. This is such a simple yet luxurious dish. It is even better served with some goat's cheese and avocado for a grown-up Sunday breakfast.

Beat the eggs and cream in a bowl using a fork.

Melt some butter in a frying pan over medium heat. Add the trout and gently break it up as it warms. After a minute or two, pour in the egg mixture and, using a spoon, gently lift and fold it a couple of times, scraping it off the bottom as you go. Pop a lid on the pan for a minute, then remove the lid and repeat the process of lifting and folding the egg mixture until it is almost cooked but still a little wet.

Remove the pan from the heat and give the mixture one more stir, then plate up and enjoy immediately.

Having a few smoothie recipes up your sleeve is essential for low-blood-sugar meltdown moments! These are great after-school snacks to sustain kids through the homework hours.

In summer, I make a bit extra and freeze leftovers in ice-cream moulds so I can offer our daughter a healthy alternative to ice-cream on hot days. Those keep her hydrated and happy.

SERVES 2

GREEN SMOOTHIE

1 cup loosely packed spinach leaves

1 fresh or frozen banana

1 avocado

Blend well with 1 cup of water, then serve.

BLUE MOON SMOOTHIE

1 cup frozen blueberries

2 free-range eggs

2 cups coconut water

1 cup coconut flesh or
½ cup desiccated coconut

Blend until smooth. Serve chilled.

CHOC CHIA THICK SHAKE

1 fresh or frozen banana

3 tablespoons chia seeds

1½ tablespoons raw cacao powder

1 cup full-fat coconut cream

1 teaspoon vanilla extract

Whizz in a blender with 1 cup of water. Serve.

NOTE FROM DAMON:
DON'T SERVE FOODS CONTAINING
RAW EGGS TO CHILDREN UNDER
2 YEARS, PREGNANT WOMEN,
PEOPLE OLDER THAN 70 YEARS
AND PEOPLE WITH LOW OR
COMPROMISED IMMUNE SYSTEMS.

RED SALAD

SERVES 4

500 g small to medium beetroot, scrubbed, trimmed and cut into halves and quarters

butter, for roasting

salt, to taste

½ cup sunflower seeds

1 × 400 g tin kidney beans, drained and rinsed

1 cup finely shredded purple cabbage

1 pomegranate, halved and seeds removed

½ cup flat-leaf parsley leaves

½ red onion, diced

2 tablespoons olive oil

juice of 1 lemon

If you want to bulk this vibrant salad up and increase the nutrient content, add 1 cup of cooked quinoa as well. You can also enjoy leftovers for breakfast as fancy pink bubble and squeak. Simply fry them up in butter, crack in one egg per person and stir through. Easy peasy.

Preheat the oven to 180°C.

Place the beetroot in a baking dish and rub it with butter and salt. Roast for 20–30 minutes or until crispy on the outside and tender on the inside. A few minutes before removing the beetroot, scatter the sunflower seeds over the top to warm and lightly toast them.

Combine all the ingredients in a salad bowl and toss well. This salad is best served warm but keeps well for lunch the following day.

VEGAN

LEFTOVERS

SALMON *and* ARTICHOKE HEART SALAD

SERVES 4

1 × 250 g jar marinated artichoke hearts, drained, oil reserved

3 × 200 g salmon fillets

⅓ cup pine nuts

100 g watercress, trimmed and torn

150 g marinated goat's cheese, drained, oil reserved

This is the first meal I ever cooked for Damon. I remember he absolutely loved it and I felt pretty chuffed with myself (as you do). It looks and tastes stunning, but it's actually really simple: the dressing comes from the oil in the artichoke hearts and the marinated goat's cheese. Damon brought a dessert (pre-sugar epiphany obviously), which we devoured afterwards, consisting of chocolate mousse, pashmak (Persian fairy floss) and chocolate-covered goji berries. You can't say we didn't know how to party – we were wild back in those days.

Add a tablespoon of the reserved artichoke oil to a small frying pan over medium heat. Fry the salmon for 10 minutes, turning halfway, until just cooked through.

In another small frying pan over medium–low heat, gently toast the pine nuts for a few minutes until they are golden and aromatic; keep them moving so they brown evenly and watch them closely so they don't burn.

Throw the watercress into a salad bowl. Cut the artichoke hearts in half and chuck them in the bowl as well. Break the salmon into pieces. Add to the bowl along with the pine nuts and goat's cheese and gently toss to combine. Serve immediately.

MARGHERITA PIZZA

MAKES 1 PIZZA

1½ tablespoons tomato paste

1 ripe tomato, chopped

6 slices mozzarella

2 cloves garlic, sliced

2–3 sprigs oregano, leaves picked, plus extra to garnish

extra virgin olive oil, for drizzling

PIZZA BASE

1 cup chickpea (besan) flour

1 teaspoon extra virgin olive oil

½ teaspoon salt

Some nights nothing else will do – you need a good movie, a cuddle on the couch and, of course, pizza. This chickpea-flour base has a lovely distinct flavour and a crispy texture. This is a pretty basic topping, but feel free to get inventive and come up with your own combos. I've always been partial to a good spicy salami myself. (Take that as you will.)

Preheat the oven to 180°C and line a large pizza tray.

For the pizza base, place the chickpea flour, oil, salt and ½ cup of water in a bowl and mix to form a dough. Spread it out over the prepared tray. Bake for 10 minutes before adding the topping.

Spread the tomato paste and chopped tomato over the pizza base using the back of a spoon. Top with the mozzarella, garlic and oregano, then drizzle with olive oil.

Bake for 15–20 minutes until the base is crispy.

NOTE FROM DAMON:
CHICKPEA (BESAN) FLOUR IS GREAT IF YOU ARE ON A WHEAT- OR GLUTEN-FREE DIET. WITH A MUCH LOWER GI THAN WHITE FLOUR, IT DELIVERS A NUTTY FLAVOUR AND A BOOST OF PROTEIN.

VEGETARIAN

HEART-OPENING GREEN SALAD

SERVES 4–6

1 cup walnut halves

1 × 400 g tin chickpeas, drained and rinsed

2 cups brussels sprouts, trimmed and very finely shredded

1 green apple, cut into matchsticks or very finely sliced using a mandoline

2 celery sticks, finely sliced

1 cup roughly chopped flat-leaf parsley

125 g goat's cheese, crumbled

1 tablespoon olive oil

Inspired by the classic Waldorf salad, this is delicious served with a simple buttery grilled or barbecued pork chop. It keeps very well too – up to 3 days in the fridge. After that, I like to cook leftovers in butter; this changes the flavour and avoids waste. This is a good little trick to have on those days when you're home alone and you need a very quick and simple lunch.

. . . .

In a large frying pan over low heat, gently toast the walnuts for 5 minutes or until they are a little crunchy and aromatic; stir them continuously to ensure they don't burn.

Combine all the ingredients in a large bowl, mix thoroughly and serve.

VEGETARIAN   LEFTOVERS

POMEGRANATE COCONUT FISH

SERVES 4, GENEROUSLY

300 g firm white fish fillets (such as monkfish), cut into 2 cm cubes

½ cup salt

2 cups water

juice of 1 lemon

juice of 1 lime

1 pomegranate, halved and seeds removed

½ cup finely diced yellow capsicum

¼ cup finely diced red onion

1 cup full-fat coconut cream

coriander leaves, to serve (optional)

This recipe is inspired by a Cook Islands dish called *ika mata*. It is similar to ceviche, which is popular right now, but the addition of coconut cream adds a new dimension. Choose firm white fish that is fresh and cheap: ask your fishmonger what's local and sustainable.

This is also the ideal summer party food as it requires no cooking and is quick to prepare. To serve it as finger food, try arranging a scoop of the fish in a lettuce or endive leaf. You can also add more vegetables if you like. Radishes work well, as do tomatoes, cucumbers and even pineapple, if you want to get really tropical!

First, soak the fish. Make a brine with the salt and water, and pour it into a non-reactive bowl. Add the fish and soak for 20 minutes.

Drain the fish and rinse the bowl. Pop the fish back in the bowl and cover with the lemon and lime juice. Leave to cure for an hour.

Transfer the fish to a serving bowl and add the pomegranate, capsicum and onion. Season with salt, then stir through the coconut cream.

Chill in the fridge before serving; this is best served very cold so, on a hot day, you may like to place the bowl in a larger bowl of ice to serve.

Sprinkle with coriander, if you like.

NOTE FROM DAMON:
POMEGRANATES ARE MOTHER NATURE'S GEMSTONES. THEY ADD A SUBTLE BURST OF NATURAL SWEETNESS TO DISHES. WE ARE VERY GOOD FRIENDS.

TUNA MELT MUSHROOMS

SERVES 4

4 large mushrooms,
such as field or portobello

2 tablespoons butter

1 × 425 g tin tuna slices
in olive oil (drained)

¾ cup roughly chopped
flat-leaf parsley

⅔ cup grated cheddar

4 large or 6 small tomatoes,
chopped

NOTE FROM DAMON:
I LAZILY ATE ONE OF THESE
THE DAY AFTER ZOE COOKED
THEM. I DIDN'T HEAT IT UP,
JUST HAD IT COLD – AND IT
WAS SURPRISINGLY DELICIOUS.
I'D HIGHLY RECOMMEND POPPING
ONE IN YOUR LUNCHBOX.

I came up with this recipe one night when all we had in the fridge were ginormous mushrooms. The conversation went something like this:

Damon: Those mushrooms . . . what do you intend to do with them?

(Uh oh.)

Me: Umm . . . Oh, the mushrooms, aren't they beautiful? I mean, look at them, they're just huge. Wow. I was going to use them for . . . umm . . .

Damon: For what?

(I frantically rummage through the cupboard while Damon looks on, dubiously.)

Me: For . . . making . . . umm . . .

(I grab a can of tuna. Aha!)

Me: Tuna mushroom melts. Yep. They'll be great.

I recommence my flurry of cupboard rummaging and then get down to business. The end result of that night surprised us both, me especially! These mega mushies were truly delicious. So clearly the moral of this story is, when you're shopping for your mushrooms, the bigger the better! Go berzerk. I dare you. While you're at it buy a few other random freakish vegetables that you may never usually buy. You might just strike gold and come up with your own accidental culinary triumph.

• •

Preheat the oven to 180°C.

Snap the stems out from the mushrooms and place a nub of butter in each cavity.

Combine the remaining ingredients in a bowl, then spoon the mixture onto the mushroom caps.

Pop them on a baking tray and bake for 30 minutes until the cheese is all melty and gooey.

VEGETARIAN   LEFTOVERS

SUMMER SALAD

SERVES 4

butter, for baking

12 baby carrots, trimmed

6 baby beetroot, scrubbed, trimmed and quartered

salt, to taste

150 g pine nuts

3 nectarines, cut into wedges

150 g goat's cheese, crumbled

This yummy recipe was on high rotation in our house for a while. Damon and I fell in love with it as it is just so easy and delicious. I say to trim the veggies here, but honestly half the time I just bung them in the oven unkempt, to add some flair (and because I'm feeling lazy!).

• •

Preheat the oven to 180°C.

Rub butter all over the carrots and beetroot and sprinkle with a little salt. Roast for 15–20 minutes or until tender.

Meanwhile, toast the pine nuts in a frying pan over medium heat for a few minutes, stirring continuously and watching them like a hawk to avoid burning, until they are aromatic and golden.

Remove the roasted veggies from the oven and arrange them on a serving platter. Scatter with the nectarine wedges, goat's cheese and toasted pine nuts. Serve warm.

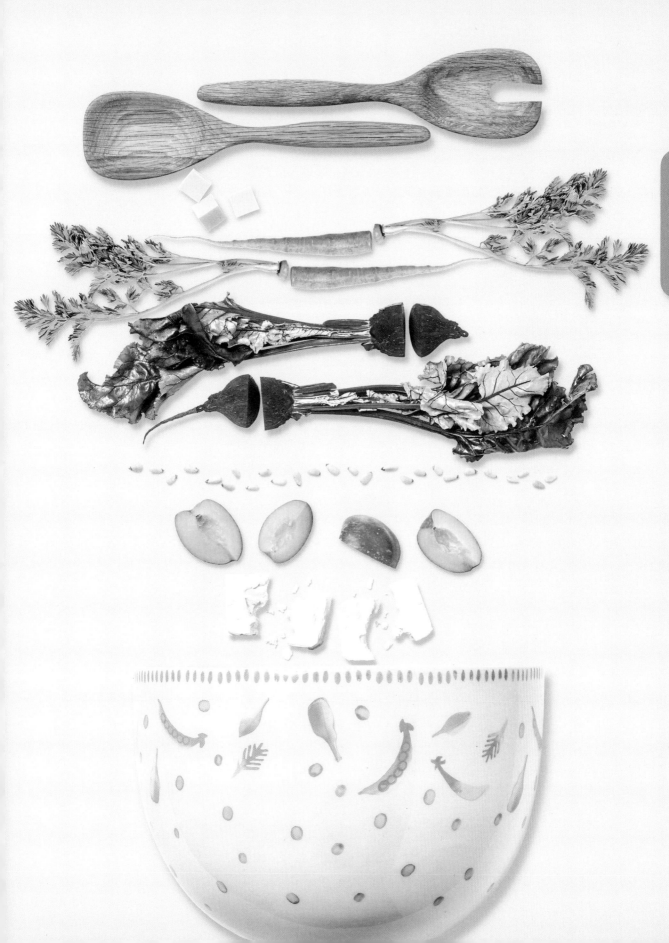

BRUSSELS SPROUT SOUP

SERVES 4

butter, for frying

6 rashers bacon, roughly chopped

500 g brussels sprouts, trimmed

1 cup thickened cream, plus extra
to serve (optional)

Damon's step-mother has been making this soup for him since he was a little boy and he still loves it. There's always some in our freezer for an emergency meal. It leaves us feeling nourished and nurtured, and wanting more every time we eat it.

Melt some butter in a large frying pan over medium heat. Add the bacon and brussels sprouts and fry for 5 minutes until they start to brown. Add 1½ cups of water and simmer for a further 10 minutes until the sprouts are tender and cooked through.

Leave to cool a little before pouring the contents of the pan into a blender. Pour in the cream and blend well until smooth.

Gently reheat before serving and finish with an additional dollop of cream, if you like.

MIDDLE EASTERN SALAD

SERVES 4

½ cup couscous

⅔ cup pine nuts

150 g haloumi, sliced

butter, for frying

1 pomegranate, halved and seeds removed (optional)

1 cup chopped mint

1 cup chopped flat-leaf parsley

1 tablespoon lemon juice

1 tablespoon ground cumin

1 tablespoon sumac

1 teaspoon salt

1 tablespoon olive oil

Damon's beautiful mother loves Middle Eastern food, so on her birthday I channelled my inner Ottolenghi and came up with this recipe. I love the combination of flavours, especially the mint and pomegranate. This is lovely served with falafel and hummus or yoghurt, or by itself. It keeps well for several days and leftovers are delicious warmed up with a little chicken cooked in butter.

Boil a kettle of water. Place the couscous in a heatproof bowl and pour over enough boiling water to cover the couscous by an extra 5 mm. Set a plate over the bowl to keep the steam in and leave for a few minutes for the couscous to absorb the water. Fluff up with a fork, then set the couscous aside.

Meanwhile, toast the pine nuts in a frying pan over medium heat for 3–5 minutes until they are aromatic and golden; keep them moving by tossing the pan and stirring, to prevent burning.

Fry the haloumi in a little butter for a couple of minutes on each side untilffigolden.

Place all the ingredients in a salad bowl and toss well to combine. Serve immediately.

VEGETARIAN   LEFTOVERS

PARSNIP FRITTERS

SERVES 4

50 g butter

2 parsnips, chopped into
1 cm cubes

1 cup walnut halves

3 cloves garlic, crushed

100 g feta

1 free-range egg

coconut oil, for frying

lemon wedges, to serve

basil leaves, to garnish (optional)

These don't sound like much but trust me they are surprisingly delicious. They are perfect for a substantial Sunday brunch, and leftovers keep for lunch the next day. You can add bacon if you wish, but the feta is salty enough that they really don't need it.

Melt half the butter in a large frying pan over low heat. Add the parsnip and walnuts. Fry lightly with the lid on for about 10 minutes until the parsnip is tender. Add the garlic and sizzle it all for a minute longer. Remove the pan from the heat and leave to cool for a minute or two.

Tip the parsnip mix into a food processor and set the frying pan aside; don't rinse it as you're about to use it again. Add the feta and egg to the food processor and pulse to roughly combine.

Shape the parsnip mixture into golf-ball-sized balls with your hands. Press down lightly to flatten, then smooth the edges. You should have about 6–8 fritters.

Add the remaining butter and some coconut oil to the pan over a high heat. Fry the fritters in batches for about 6 minutes, turning halfway, until they are crunchy and golden on the outside and the egg is cooked through.

Serve with lemon wedges and some basil to garnish, if you like.

NOTE FROM DAMON:
THESE ARE A KNOCKOUT
AND MAKE BRILLIANT
LUNCHBOX SNACKS FOR
KIDS AND ADULTS ALIKE.

CHICKEN SCHNITZELS

SERVES 6

1 kg chicken breasts

1 cup tapioca or arrowroot flour

4 free-range eggs,
plus extra if needed

1½ cups fine desiccated coconut

2 cups almond meal

1½ cups finely grated parmesan

2–3 cups coconut oil

lemon wedges, to serve

Fennel and Cabbage Salad
(see page 206) or steamed
broccoli, to serve

NOTE FOR DAMON:
USE VEAL INSTEAD OF
CHICKEN FOR VARIATION. THE
FLAVOUR WORKS BRILLIANTLY
WITH THE ALMOND MEAL. I
PREFER VEAL, ACTUALLY, BUT
CHICKEN IS EASIER TO COME
BY AND MORE AFFORDABLE.

This is one of my all-time favourite recipes, based on the breadcrumb version my mama cooks – she is the schnitzel queen. Kids used to raid my lunchbox on schnitzel day, they were that good. The key to her successful perfect crunch was double-crumbing the schnitzels and I swear it's the difference between a ho–hum schnitz and the real mouthwatering deal! Schnitzel-making can be a messy and time-consuming process, so make a few extra schnitzels to freeze for another time.

You can easily turn the schnitzels into parmigianas by adding tomato sauce, ham and cheese on top and baking them in the oven until the cheese melts.

Preheat the oven on the lowest setting – just enough to keep the schnitzels warm. Cut your chicken breasts in half lengthways and, using a meat mallet, pound them until they are about 5 mm thick; it doesn't matter if they end up with holey patches.

Place the flour in a shallow bowl. Beat the eggs in a large bowl. Mix the desiccated coconut, almond meal and parmesan together in another large bowl and set it beside the egg plate. Place another large plate beside the crumb bowl and start your schnitzing! Dip your chicken into the flour, then dip it into the egg and coat it, allowing any excess to drip off. Dip it into the crumb mix, coating really well and pressing the crumbs to stick. Lay the crumbed schnitzel on the plate and repeat with the remaining chicken.

Heat the coconut oil in a large frying pan over a low heat. Line a baking tray with baking paper and place it beside the pan. Repeat the crumbing process a second time with the chicken pieces; just a loose coat will do. You may need to add an additional egg or two to the egg wash. Keep crumbing process until you run out of the crumb mix.

Turn the heat to medium. Test the temperature by dropping in a bit of crumb; if it sizzles, the oil is hot and ready to go. Working in batches of 2 or 3, carefully add the schnitzels. Fry on one side for a few minutes until the crumbs turn golden, then flip them over to cook the other side. Remove them and drain them on paper towel. Pop them into the oven to stay warm while you cook the rest. Serve immediately with lemon wedges and fennel salad or steamed broccoli on the side.

LEFTOVERS   OCCASIONAL FOODS

PORK CASSEROLE

**SERVES 6
WITH LEFTOVERS**

1 kg pork cutlets, fat on

butter, for browning

1 onion, diced

½ cup sage leaves

½ cup finely chopped parsnip

½ cup finely chopped carrot

¼ cup apple cider vinegar

1 × 400 g tin lima beans
(butter beans), drained and rinsed

2 pears, cored and quartered

2 cups coconut water

This casserole can be made easily in a slow cooker and left for the day. It is a welcoming and delicious-smelling meal to come home to. If you don't have a slow cooker, you can use a large casserole dish instead. Fennel and Cabbage Salad works nicely with this (see page 206).

· ·

In your slow cooker or casserole dish, brown the cutlets in the butter over high heat for a minute each side. Add the onion and sage and let them sizzle for a moment. Add the parsnip, carrot and vinegar, then tip in the rest of the ingredients and pop the lid on.

Leave the pork casserole to slow-cook for the day (I use a high setting and leave it to cook for 6–8 hours) or place the casserole dish in a 130°C oven and cook for 7 hours, checking the water level occasionally.

LEFTOVERS OCCASIONAL FOODS

TRUE-BLUE SLOW-COOKED LAMB

SERVES 6, GENEROUSLY

100 g butter, softened

150 g blue cheese

5 cloves garlic, crushed

2 kg lamb shoulder, bone in

green leaves, to serve

CUMIN SALT

2 tablespoons ground cumin

2 tablespoons salt

This lamb shoulder is the easiest show-stopper around. A friend introduced me to the recipe a long time ago and since then I have slightly adjusted it and whipped it up at many a cook-off over the years. The blue cheese and butter replicate a Moroccan fermented butter called *smen*. It's basically impressive simple street food.

Preheat the oven to 120°C.

Combine the butter, blue cheese and garlic to make a paste, then slather it all over the lamb.

Place the shoulder in a large casserole dish and add 1 cup of water to keep the lamb moist. Pop the lid on and roast the lamb for 6–8 hours, checking it once after 3 hours to make sure it's still moist, adding up to a cup of water if needed.

About 30–40 minutes before the end of the cooking time, remove the foil and turn the oven up to 180°C to brown the lamb. The lamb is ready when it falls off the bone with the gentle prod of a fork.

For the cumin salt, simply mix the ingredients together.

Scatter the green leaves over the lamb and serve with cumin salt for sprinkling.

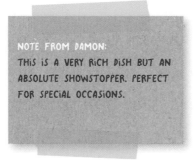

NOTE FROM DAMON:
THIS IS A VERY RICH DISH BUT AN
ABSOLUTE SHOWSTOPPER. PERFECT
FOR SPECIAL OCCASIONS.

LEFTOVERS   OCCASIONAL FOODS

EASY CHEESY CABBAGE BAKE

SERVES 2–4

1 white cabbage, cut in half top to bottom

1½ cups thickened cream

100 g blue cheese, crumbled

I like to make this as a side dish, in lieu of potato gratin – it captures the same creaminess and warmth, but without the heaviness. I especially enjoy it alongside a simple lemony roast chook.

Preheat the oven to 180°C and line a baking tray with foil.

Make a cross on the cut side of the cabbage halves taking care not to cut through completely. Gently pull apart to loosen the leaves without splitting them. Place on the prepared tray.

Drizzle the cream into the cabbage halves and sprinkle with blue cheese.

Bake for about 30 minutes or until the cabbage is tender and the cheese has melted.

VEGETARIAN

SELF-SAUCED BANGERS *and* CAULIFLOWER CHEESE

SERVES 4

butter, for frying

8 large beef sausages

3 cloves garlic, sliced

1 teaspoon ground black pepper

1 × 400 g tin diced tomatoes

CAULIFLOWER CHEESE

300 g cauliflower florets

½ cup pouring cream

1 cup fresh drained ricotta

1 cup grated parmesan

salt and pepper, to taste

Our neighbour Estelle is incredible. A mum of three who runs her own business from home, she was a huge source of inspiration to me when I was writing these recipes. I would ask myself: would Estelle have time to make this? Is it affordable for a family of five like Estelle's? Would Estelle be able to cook this while juggling a toddler on one hip, a three-year-old having a meltdown, a hungry teen and a hubby about to burst through the door?

What's more, I tested a few recipes out on her and the kids and I can happily reveal they got the thumbs up!

The light tomato sauce here is similar to one Estelle cooks. It replaces commercial sauce, which is usually full of sugar, and adds oomph and moisture.

I used plain pure-meat beef sausages for this recipe, but pork, lamb and chicken work well too.

Preheat the oven to 180°C. Line a 30 × 20 cm baking dish with baking paper.

To make the cauliflower cheese, arrange the cauli in the baking dish, top with the cream and ricotta and sprinkle with parmesan. Bake for 30 minutes or until golden and crispy on top.

Meanwhile, melt a little butter in a large frying pan over medium heat. Fry the sausages for 10 minutes, turning every so often, until they are browning nicely on the outside but still a little raw in the middle. Throw in the garlic and pepper and fry for another minute, then tip the tomatoes over the top and pop the lid on the pan. Cook for a further 10 minutes or so until the sausages are cooked through and the tomato sauce has thickened a little.

To serve, place some cauliflower cheese on each plate with a couple of sausages beside it and spoon the sauce over the top.

LEFTOVERS   TODDLER FRIENDLY

SLOW-COOKED COCONUT CHICKEN

SERVES 4–6,
WITH LEFTOVERS

1 large young coconut

1 × 1.5 kg whole chicken

2 celery sticks, chopped

4 large carrots,
cut into 2.5 cm pieces

300 g pumpkin,
roughly chopped

3 cloves garlic (whole)

⅓ cup lemon juice

400 g green beans,
topped and tailed

In the early days of breastfeeding, I always had a pot of this on the go – it provided a wonderful steady stream of hydration and nourishment. The coconut chicken broth made from slow-cooking in this way is so rich yet still light. You can use the leftover broth for soup stock or drink it on its own as a hearty winter warmer: it's a great immunity booster. You can also turn the leftover chicken into muffins (see page 70). I've used pumpkin, carrot and green beans here but feel free to vary the veggies.

Crack and drain the coconut water into a bowl, then scoop out 1 cup of coconut flesh. You want about 2 cups of coconut water; if you don't have enough, top it up to this amount with water.

Rinse and pat dry the chicken, then place it in a slow cooker. Scatter the celery, carrot, pumpkin, garlic and coconut flesh around the chicken, then cover it with the lemon juice, coconut water and an extra 1 cup of water.

Cook for 3 hours on a high setting or 6 hours or more on a low setting. About 10–12 minutes before serving, add the green beans and cook until just tender.

Serve the chicken and vegetables with the broth in soup bowls.

LEFTOVERS   TODDLER FRIENDLY

CHICKEN, CHEESE *and* LEEK PIE

SERVES 4–6

butter, for frying and greasing

600 g chicken thigh fillets, cut into bite-sized pieces

2 large leeks, thinly sliced

1 tablespoon apple cider vinegar

½ cup thickened cream

1½ cups grated cheddar

steamed broccoli, to serve

PASTRY

2 eggs

2 cups fine almond meal

1 tablespoon coconut oil

1 teaspoon salt

I first made this pie on a night Damon's dad and step-mum were over for dinner. I'd never made pastry before – certainly not an almond meal crust – or a flourless pie filling, and there I was making both, from scratch, for guests expecting real food, not a science experiment! Somehow I managed to pull it off and the four of us polished the whole pie off in one sitting. The cheese layer under the crust makes it extra tasty and stops the crust becoming soggy and saggy. Definitely worth stepping out of your comfort zone and into homemade pastry land for!

Preheat the oven to 180°C and grease a pie dish (ours is 20 cm round) with butter.

In a large frying pan, melt the butter over high heat and brown the chicken for a couple of minutes, turning to brown evenly. Add the leek and vinegar, then turn down the heat and pop on the lid; this will keep in the moisture. Gently cook for a further 10 minutes, stirring occasionally to prevent the chicken from sticking to the pan. Add the cream and ½ cup of the cheese to the chicken and stir it through to combine. Immediately remove the pan from the heat and set it aside, with the lid.

Meanwhile, to make the pastry, place 1 egg and the remaining ingredients in a food processor and whizz them together until well combined. Form the dough into a large ball. Tear off some baking paper and plonk the ball onto it, pressing it down a little so it starts to flatten. Lay a second sheet of baking paper on top and roll out the dough until it is about 1 cm thick. Set the pastry aside (in the fridge if you're preparing it in advance).

Tip the chicken out of the frying pan into the pie dish and sprinkle over the remaining cheese. Lay the pastry on top and trim the edges, leaving some pastry hanging over the sides. Using a knife, poke a little hole in the centre to allow the steam to escape during cooking. Lightly beat the remaining egg and brush it over the top of the pastry.

Pop the pie in the oven and bake for 25–30 minutes until the crust is golden. Serve immediately with some steamed broccoli for green goodness.

LEFTOVERS

MEXICAN CHICKEN SALAD BOWL

**SERVES 2 AS A MAIN
OR 4 AS A SIDE**

butter, for frying

1 small onion, sliced

2 cloves garlic, sliced

2 tablespoons dried oregano

½ tablespoon paprika

½ tablespoon ground cumin

2 chicken breasts

2 tablespoons apple cider vinegar

2 small red capsicums, seeded
and chopped

4 tomatoes, roughly chopped

1 × 400 g tin black beans, drained
and rinsed

2 corn cobs

1 avocado, roughly chopped

chopped iceberg lettuce,
to serve (optional)

sour cream, to serve (optional)

lime wedges, to serve (optional)

This recipe was inspired by a salad bowl we ate in a fast food joint in the States, a place called Chipotle. Arriving in the middle of nowhere jetlagged and starving, we were prepared to compromise and eat whatever was available, when this little gem emerged like a mirage in a desert of terrible chains, with their salad bowls and sustainably farmed meat. This recipe is my interpretation of that meal – enjoy.

Melt the butter in a large frying pan over medium heat. Add the onion and garlic and fry for a couple of minutes to soften, then throw in the oregano, paprika and cumin to warm for a minute. Add the chicken breasts and splash the apple cider vinegar all over, then add the capsicum and tomato and stir the mixture together. Turn the heat down to low and simmer for 10 minutes or until the chicken is cooked through but still moist; add up to ½ cup of water if needed during cooking.

Place the black beans in a large salad bowl. Cut the corn from the cob and add it to the beans. Once the chicken is cooked, shred it with a fork, then add it and the sauce to the beans and corn. Tip the avocado over the top, then give it all a good toss to combine.

Serve as is or with iceberg lettuce, sour cream and a squeeze of lime over the top.

VEGETARIAN BAKE

SERVES 4–6

butter, for frying

600 g pumpkin,
peeled and thinly sliced

2½ cups grated cheddar

2 eggplants, thinly sliced

1 cup Cultured 'Cream Cheese'
(see page 119) or use good-quality
shop-bought

2 large zucchini, sliced

1½ tablespoons salt

400 g fresh ricotta, drained

SAUCE

butter, for frying

3 cloves garlic, crushed

500 g mushrooms, finely chopped

3 tablespoons apple cider vinegar

2 × 400 g tins diced tomatoes

salt, to taste

TOPPING

½ cup grated cheddar

½ cup almond meal

Similar to a lasagne, this bake is a little time consuming to make, but it's worth it especially when you double the ingredients to make a freezer batch as well. If your family is used to the traditional lasagne with pasta layers and misses this component then try inserting a couple of layers of mountain bread between the vegetable layers instead of the pasta sheets. Mountain bread is not only thinner than traditional pasta but comes in many varieties, including low gluten, low GI and wholegrain.

Preheat the oven to 180°C. Grease a large baking dish (ours is 40 × 30 cm) and place it next to your stovetop, ready for the layers of vegetables.

To make the sauce, melt some butter in a large saucepan over high heat and add the garlic and mushrooms. Fry for a minute or two until softened, then add the vinegar and tomatoes and bring to a simmer. Reduce the heat to low and pop the lid on to let it cook away while you prepare the vegetable layers.

Melt some butter in a large frying pan over medium heat. Add half the pumpkin slices or enough to make one layer in your baking dish and fry for 5 minutes with the lid on; shake the pan and stir occasionally to prevent the pumpkin from sticking. Transfer the par-cooked pumpkin to the baking dish. Spread 2 heaped tablespoons of the tomato sauce over the pumpkin layer, then sprinkle it with cheddar. Next, add enough eggplant slices to make a second layer and fry for 10 minutes until starting to soften, turning halfway. Layer the eggplant slices over the cheese, then spoon over some tomato sauce and dollop with cream cheese. Add the zucchini and another tiny blob of butter to the pan and fry for 5 minutes until starting to soften. Transfer to the baking dish, spoon over some sauce and top with a layer of ricotta. Continue layering until all the veggies, sauce and cheeses have been used up. (When you get to the top layers, you may have to combine vegetables.)

To make the topping, combine the cheddar and almond meal and sprinkle evenly over the final layer of vegetables. Haul the big baking dish into the oven and bake for 40 minutes or until the top is golden and crunchy.

Serve hot with a green salad, if you like. Store it in the fridge and reheat it before serving the next day.

VEGETARIAN   LEFTOVERS

SUMAC STEAK *with* ALMOND-CRUSTED BROCCOLI

SERVES 2

1 tablespoon butter

2 × 200 g fillet steaks

2 teaspoons sumac

ALMOND-CRUSTED BROCCOLI

300 g broccoli,
chopped into florets

1 tablespoon seeded mustard

1 cup almond meal

½ cup grated parmesan

This is my favourite way to eat steak. The sumac adds wonderful zing and flavour. For the best results, bring the steak to room temperature before cooking: I've found this can make even cheap cuts more tender. The almond-crusted broccoli is a tasty and verstaile side. Lots of people believe broccoli has to be steamed or boiled until squishy, but I'm a big fan of serving it roasted or even raw – give it a try. Any leftover almond-crusted broccoli can be eaten for lunch with a side salad the next day.

• •

Preheat the oven to 180°C and line a baking tray with baking paper.

Scatter the broccoli florets on the prepared tray and roll them in seeded mustard to coat. Sprinkle with the almond meal and then the parmesan. Roast in the oven for 15 minutes until crunchy and golden.

Meanwhile, heat a frying pan over high heat until it's really hot, then throw in the butter and let it sizzle. Immediately put the steaks in the pan and cook for 3 minutes, then flip them over and sprinkle with sumac. Cook for another few minutes, depending on your preferred taste and the thickness of the steaks.

Serve the steaks with the almond-crusted broccoli.

LEFTOVERS

CAULIFLOWER *and* TUNA MORNAY

SERVES 4

butter, for frying and baking

400 g cauliflower florets

½ cup thickened cream

250 g fresh ricotta, drained

1 cup grated cheddar

1 cup sweetcorn

1 × 425 g tin tuna, drained

½ cup grated parmesan

Ideal comfort food. This is such a family favourite, I knew I had to attempt a low-carb, sugar-free version. I promise you won't miss the potato at all – the flavour is spot on without it. I like to use the fan-forced setting on my oven when I make this recipe as it works better at absorbing the moisture in the dish. This is lovely served with a simple green salad.

Preheat the oven to 180°C (fan-forced) and grease a small baking dish with butter.

Melt some butter in a frying pan over medium heat and add the cauliflower and cream. Pop the lid on and cook for 15 minutes or until the cauli florets are tender.

While the cauli and cream are gently bubbling away, place the ricotta, cheddar, corn and tuna in a bowl and stir them together. Transfer the mixture to the baking dish.

Spoon half of the cauliflower florets over the tuna mixture. Mash the remaining cauliflower and cream until smooth, then pour it over the top. Finally, sprinkle over the parmesan.

Pop the mornay in the oven and bake for 30 minutes or so until the top begins to look golden and crunchy.

LEFTOVERS

THE SUGAR-FREE NAG'S HUSBAND-FRIENDLY BBQ RIBS

SERVES 4, GENEROUSLY

2 kg pork American-style ribs
(4 sides)

2 tablespoons apple cider vinegar
or water

220 g tomato paste
(check for no added sugar)

1 really ripe large nectarine
or peach, stone removed, roughly
chopped

6 large or 8 small blackberries

1 tablespoon chopped oregano

1 tablespoon paprika

1 teaspoon salt

This recipe was created with all the sugar-free nags in mind. You've seen the film but your family is dubious about incorporating your newfound values into your shared mealtimes. This is a great starting point to get the husband onside at least! Don't tell him until after he's devoured it that the sauce is homemade. This is not an everyday meal or even a weekly meal, but an impressive dish that can be enjoyed on a rare occasion by the sugary and sugar-free alike.

For variety every now and then, try using plums or cherries in the marinade instead of nectarines and blackberries. And for a lighter snack, you could switch the ribs for chicken wings; they can be marinated within 30 minutes and cooked in about 15 minutes at 180°C. These ribs are particularly delicious served alongside green leaves with a light lemony dressing to cut through the richness.

• •

Rinse and dry the ribs, then cut them into sections of about 4 or 5 ribs per person.

Combine all the remaining ingredients in a blender and whizz on high until a smooth thick paste is formed.

Line a large baking tray with baking paper. Spread a third of the paste over the prepared tray and lay the ribs on top. Smother the top of the ribs with the remaining sauce. Cover them loosely with foil and seal the edges so limited moisture escapes during cooking. Leave at room temperature to marinate for 2 hours. Or, if you're preparing the ribs the day before, place them in the fridge to marinate overnight. Return the ribs to room temperature an hour before roasting.

Preheat the oven to 140°C (I don't recommend using a fan-forced oven for this recipe, as it tends to dry out the ribs.) Pop the marinated ribs in the oven for about 2 hours. Remove the foil covering and check the ribs are tender and cooked through. Increase the oven temp to 180°C and return the ribs, uncovered, to the oven for a further 10–15 minutes to give them a bit of extra oomph. Make sure you check them as the fruit in the sauce can cause them to brown very quickly. The ribs should be succulent and tender and oh so tasty.

LEFTOVERS   OCCASIONAL FOODS

TATTIE'S PATTIES

MAKES 12

1 tablespoon coconut oil,
plus extra for greasing

600 g chicken breast fillets,
roughly chopped

3 tablespoons roughly chopped
lemon and its juice

1 clove garlic, crushed

1 teaspoon dried thyme

1 teaspoon paprika

1 teaspoon salt

lettuce leaves and lime wedges, to
serve (optional)

Roasted Pumpkin with Dukkah
(see page 207), to serve (optional)

This recipe is inspired by a dear English friend of mine. She makes these simple yet delicious chicken patties for her nephews, who call her Tattie instead of Auntie . . . hence the name Tattie's Patties! I've tweaked the original recipe a little to make it toddler friendly for those with more gum and less tooth! And I've added coconut oil, which I love.

The patties may seem wet when you handle them raw but they'll cook up superbly, I promise. I find baking them in the oven can be a cleaner method than frying when you're in a rush and have other things to prepare. If you prefer the fried flavour though, go ahead and cook them in batches in a frying pan. This recipe can easily be doubled and leftovers make good lunchbox snacks. One last tip: if you feel like mixing it up, try using turkey fillets instead of chicken. Wild, I know – my thrills are cheap.

Preheat the oven to 180°C. Line a baking tray with baking paper and grease with coconut oil.

Place the chicken in a food processor with the lemon, garlic, thyme, paprika and salt and pulse until the chicken is finely ground and everything is well combined.

Form the mixture into about 12 patties, flopping them onto the prepared tray as you go, then flatten them out with the back of a fork.

Bung them in the oven; they should be done in about 10–15 minutes tops. If you like, serve in lettuce leaves with lime wedges, or with roasted pumpkin.

LEFTOVERS   TODDLER FRIENDLY

ROASTED PUMPKIN
with **DUKKAH**
(see page 207)

SIMPLE BRUSSELS SPROUTS
(see page 206)

FENNEL *and* CABBAGE SALAD
(see page 206)

FENNEL AND CABBAGE SALAD

SERVES 4–6

1 cup finely shredded fennel (reserve the fronds for garnish, if you like)

1 cup finely shredded red cabbage

1 green apple, finely sliced, skin, seeds and all

juice of 1 lemon

1 tablespoon olive oil

1 teaspoon seeded mild mustard

This salad is quickly prepared using a mandoline but just as easy to make by cutting the veggies up finely with a good sharp knife. The lightness of this salad complements the heavier meat dishes such as the True-Blue Slow-cooked Lamb on page 186. It also soaks up the juices of a casserole dish such as the Coconut Chicken on page 190.

Combine the shredded fennel, cabbage and apple in a serving bowl.

In a small jar, combine the lemon juice, olive oil and mustard, then pop the lid on and shake vigorously to combine. Tip the dressing over the salad and serve immediately.

VEGETARIAN

SIMPLE BRUSSELS SPROUTS

SERVES 4

400 g brussels sprouts, trimmed and halved

butter, for frying

2 cloves garlic, crushed

1 teaspoon black pepper

lemon wedges, to serve

This is the perfect accompaniment to Chicken Schnitzel (see page 182). Brussel sprouts are a much maligned vegetable but I am determined to reveal how versatile and delicious they can be. Their natural flavour when cooked is quite buttery anyway, so this recipe here is just to enhance that and give them a little more oomph.

Bring a small saucepan of water to the boil over high heat.

Pop the sprouts into the boiling water and turn the heat down to medium. Let them simmer away for 15 minutes until they are softened but still a vibrant green. Drain and transfer the brussels sprouts to a bowl for serving.

Return the saucepan to the heat and melt some over a low heat. Add the garlic, then the pepper and cook, stirring, for 3 minutes until the garlic is aromatic. Turn the heat off and add some more butter to the pan, stirring briskly until it just melts. Pour the buttery garlic mix over the brussels sprouts and serve immediately with lemon wedges, if you like.

VEGETARIAN

ROASTED PUMPKIN *with* DUKKAH

SERVES 6

1 whole (600 g) jap pumpkin,
skin on

DUKKAH

½ cup hazelnuts

½ cup sesame seeds

1 teaspoon ground cumin

1 teaspoon sumac

1 tablespoon chia seeds

½ teaspoon ground cinnamon

½ teaspoon ground turmeric

olive oil, for drizzling

This is a great simple side to serve as an accompaniment to meat. You could also scatter 100 g of goat's cheese on top as well as the dukkah and serve it as the main feature in a vegetarian meal.

Preheat the oven to 180°C. Place the pumpkin on a baking tray and roast for up to 2 hours or until the skin is starting to blacken.

For the dukkah, pulse the hazelnuts in a food processor for 2 minutes until ground. Then add the sesame seeds, cumin, sumac, chia seeds, cinnamon and turmeric. Pulse together for another minute to combine well.

Remove the pumpkin from the oven and set aside for 5 minutes to cool slightly. Using a tea towel to protect your hands as needed, gently peel away the burnt skin and split apart the pumpkin with your hands to make a rough mess of it on the tray and reveal the seeds inside. Use a large metal spoon to scoop out the seeds.

Transfer the whole pumpkin with the skin on the underside to a serving platter. Scatter it with the dukkah and drizzle olive oil over the top to finish.

VEGAN

SPICED ALMONDS
and **OLIVES WITH GARLIC**
(see page 211)

GUACAMOLE
(see page 211)

KALE CHIPS
(see page 210)

FRIED TEMPEH *and* **CHORIZO**
(see page 210)

FRIED TEMPEH *and* CHORIZO

SERVES 2

150 g tempeh

150 g chorizo

butter, for frying

My mama came up with this combination when she stayed with us after Velvet was born. The fridge was almost bare, so she got inventive and struck gold with this winner.

....

Slice the tempeh and chorizo into pieces of a similar shape and size.

Fry them gently in a little butter, stirring, for about 5 minutes until the chorizo is crisp and the tempeh is browned.

KALE CHIPS

SERVES 4

1 bunch curly kale, stems removed, leaves torn into chip-sized pieces

2 tablespoons coconut oil, melted

1 teaspoon salt

Let's face it: kale may be trendy but it can be a little tough in texture. However, cooked this way it is completely delicious and moreish.

....

Preheat the oven to 150°C and line two baking trays with baking paper.

Rub the kale all over with the oil and salt, and spread out over the prepared trays.

Bake the kale chips for about 7 minutes or until the edges just start to brown. They are best served immediately but will keep in an airtight container or sealed paper bag for a snack the next day.

VEGETARIAN

SPICED ALMONDS *and* OLIVES WITH GARLIC

SERVES 4–6

1 tablespoon olive oil

1 cup almonds

1 teaspoon ground cumin

½ teaspoon salt

2 cloves garlic, finely sliced

1 cup olives

These are excellent served with a pre-dinner drink. You can use any olives of your choosing – I like mixed batches or Sicilian olives.

. . . .

Gently warm the olive oil in a large frying pan over low heat. Add the almonds, then the cumin and salt and toast gently, stirring for 3–5 minutes. Once the almonds are a little crispy and plump, add the garlic and stir for a minute. Finally, add the olives and heat for another couple of minutes, stirring all the while.

Serve warm.

VEGAN

GUACAMOLE

SERVES 8 WITH DIPPERS

2 ripe avocados

½–1 cup torn coriander leaves

juice of 1 lime

juice of ½ lemon

1 teaspoon salt

1 teaspoon paprika

3 tablespoons finely diced red onion

Before I met Damon, I lived in an apartment block in Sydney's Bronte. My American neighbour, Sue, taught me how to make guacamole, telling me 'Don't put garlic in it – that's the mistake everyone makes!' I think she was right: it is so much lighter and fresher without it. I remember her every time I make this recipe. You can vary the amount of coriander according to your family's tastes. Damon says he doesn't like it, but I sometimes sneak some in and he doesn't notice . . .

. . . .

Throw all the ingredients in a bowl and smash them together with a fork to combine.

Serve with veggie sticks or as a side to some grilled chicken or beef.

VEGAN

LEMON *and* THYME MUSHROOMS

SERVES 4

500 g button mushrooms

1 tablespoon butter

3 tablespoons thyme leaves
(or 1 tablespoon dried thyme), plus
extra sprigs to garnish (optional)

1½ tablespoons lemon juice

salt, to taste

This recipe is based on my memory of a dish served by my friend's
mother when I was in high school. Not being a mushroom fan, I was
very dubious, but I decided to be brave and try one . . . then nearly ate
the whole lot. The next day, my friend had the leftovers for lunch and
they were almost better than they'd been the night before! So if you
are not yet a shroom fan, these may well be the magic mushrooms
you've been waiting for! These couldn't be easier to make, and are
a perfect dinner-party entree.

. . . .

Rinse the mushrooms well, leaving the stalks on. Drain, but don't dry
the mushrooms as the additional moisture is good for this dish.

Melt the butter in a large lidded frying pan over medium heat. Add
the mushrooms, thyme and lemon juice, and season with salt, then
reduce the heat, pop the lid on and cook for about 8 minutes, stirring
regularly. You may need to add up to ⅓ cup of water to prevent the
mushrooms from sticking.

Serve in a large bowl with any juices poured over the top and thyme sprigs
to garnish, if you like..

VEGETARIAN   LEFTOVERS

SWEET POTATO MINI PIZZAS

SERVES 4

1 large fat sweet potato, thinly sliced into rounds

coconut oil, for baking

salt, to taste

150 g mozzarella, thinly sliced into rounds

150 g tomatoes, thinly sliced

1 cup basil leaves

cracked black pepper, to taste

A fun post-school snack, especially good for cooler evenings.

Preheat the oven to 180°C and line a large baking tray with baking paper.

Place the sweet potato rounds on the prepared tray and sprinkle with a little coconut oil and salt. Bake for 15 minutes until the sweet potato is cooked through.

Arrange the sweet potato rounds on a serving plate and top with mozzarella and tomato. Sprinkle with basil and cracked black pepper, to serve.

VEGETARIAN

FRUIT *and* CHEESE BOARD

SERVES 4

100 g cheddar

100 g brie or camembert

1 apple, thinly sliced into rounds

1 pear, thinly sliced

An easy afternoon snack to tide you over until dinner. We often use fruit instead of crackers; it's good with dips as well.

. . . .

Arrange all your ingredients on a bread board and leave on the kitchen bench for people to snack on as they pass through.

WARMED BRIE

SERVES 4

1 × 300 g wheel of brie

½ cup assorted chopped herbs (optional)

In my dark and dangerous days pre-Damon I had a French boyfriend who made this when he was feeling homesick. In those days, I ate it with a crusty baguette, but it is fantastic served with the Parsnip Chips on page 95 as dippers. Thyme, oregano and parsley all work nicely here.

. . . .

Preheat the oven to 180°C.

Cut a circle into the top white layer of your brie wheel, leaving the rim intact so it holds the soft cheesy centre. Sprinkle your herbs into the cavity.

Pop the brie onto a baking tray. Bake for 10 minutes or so until the cheese is warmed through and melty in the middle and slightly bubbly on the top.

CHILD *of* THE EIGHTIES: CELERY *and* PEANUT BUTTER BOATS

SERVES 2

2 celery sticks, trimmed of leaves

4 tablespoons sugar-free peanut butter

Fot me, these super-simple snacks are synonymous with my childhood – every time I visited friends' houses, parents would make these for us to munch on. I want to bring them back into the mainstream where they belong!

Just fill the celery with peanut butter and eat!

VEGAN

CHIA CACAO PUDDING

SERVES 4

1 × 400 ml tin full-fat coconut cream

½ cup raw cacao powder

⅓ cup chia seeds

½ banana

mixed berries, to serve (optional)

An easy one to make in advance, then whip out of the fridge at a relaxed dinner party. We used to have dinner parties once upon a time. Now we are lucky if we see the sun set before bedtime, we are that boring and parenty!

You can be creative with the serving dishes here. I like to use tea cups, little jars, small dessert bowls or glasses.

• •

Whizz all the ingredients in a blender until smooth and frothy.

Pour into serving containers and pop in the fridge to firm up; this takes between 2 to 4 hours depending on the size of the dishes. If you need to store them, put them in an airtight container or cover the dish with plastic film. They'll keep in the fridge for a couple of days.

Serve straight from the fridge with mixed berries, if using.

VEGAN

BANANA, LIME *and* COCONUT MACAROONS

MAKES ABOUT 28

3 cups shredded coconut

½ banana

½ tablespoon lime juice

1 teaspoon vanilla extract

3 tablespoons full-fat coconut milk

6 free-range egg whites

⅓ teaspoon salt

1 tablespoon grated lime zest

These delicate morsels are delightful served for a baby or bridal shower. I'm fairly sure these are the kinds of things fairies eat in their magical little kingdoms . . .

Preheat the oven to 180°C and line a baking tray with baking paper.

Put the shredded coconut into a large bowl. Place the banana, lime juice, vanilla and coconut milk in a food processor and whizz to combine. Transfer to the bowl of coconut and stir well to combine.

In a large bowl, whisk the egg whites and salt until stiff peaks form. Lightly fold the coconut banana mixture through the egg whites.

Using a serving spoon, scoop out the mixture onto the prepared tray to form little mounds just smaller than golf balls. Sprinkle some lime zest on top. Bake for 15–20 minutes or until the macaroons are starting to turn golden on top. Eat warm or leave to cool and store in an airtight container.

VEGETARIAN   LEFTOVERS

CHOC MANGO CHEEKS

MAKES 12

3 ripe juicy mangoes

1 medjool date, pitted

⅓ cup raw cacao powder

100 g cacao butter

So easy and so delicious. This is best made in summer when mangoes are in season. Buy a tray and once they are really ripe make a few batches to store in the freezer in airtight containers. They will keep for a couple of months.

Skin the mangoes and cut the cheeks off (sounds gruesome, doesn't it?). Cut the cheeks in half again, then skewer them with paddle-pop sticks in one end delicately to make an 'ice block'. Place them on a baking tray and pop them in the freezer for at least 15 minutes while you prepare the cacao coating.

Soak the date in enough water to cover for at least 4 hours. Discard the soaking water.

Melt the cacao butter by gradually adding little pieces to a saucepan over a very low heat; you'll need about 1 cup of melted cacao butter. Transfer to a blender along with the cacao powder and soaked date and whizz until completely smooth. Transfer to a bowl.

Remove the mangoes from the freezer and dip them into the cacao. Return them to the tray and into the freezer for a further 15 minutes. If you want to, you can repeat this last step of the process for a double layer of cacao crunch. Leave them frozen until ready for serving. These should keep for up to a month in the freezer but you might want to transfer them to a container to stop them getting overly frosty. You can individually portion them in baking paper tied with string, if you like, which keeps them very well. Pop them in an airtight container and freeze them until required.

VEGAN   TODDLER FRIENDLY

AVOCADO *and* COCONUT ICE-CREAM *with* DATE-CACAO COATING

MAKES 6

2 medjool dates, pitted

1 large ripe avocado

1 × 400 ml tin full-fat coconut cream

100 g cacao butter

⅓ cup raw cacao powder

These amazing ice-creams are sweetened with dates and are so creamy and decadent. They are so good to have on hand if you're a former sweet tooth who still gets the occasional craving. They will keep for up to a month in the freezer but you'll probably polish them off within days, to be honest!

Soak the dates in enough water to cover for at least 4 hours. Discard the soaking water.

Place one of the soaked dates in a blender with the avocado and coconut cream and whizz until smooth and light. Pour into 6 ice–cream moulds and freeze 4–5 hours until solid, preferably overnight.

The next day, melt the cacao butter by gradually adding it to a heatproof bowl set over a pan of gently simmering water (make sure the bowl doesn't touch the water). You want to end up with 1 cup of melted cacao butter.

Place the melted cacao butter, cacao powder and remaining soaked date in a blender and whizz until completely smooth. Transfer to a bowl.

Line a baking tray with baking paper. Remove the frozen ice-creams from the moulds by briefly running the moulds under warm water. Place them on the prepared tray.

Drizzle or dip the popsicles with half the cacao mixture and return to the freezer immediately.

Once the cacao layer is frozen solid (about 1 hour), repeat with a second coat of cacao mixture. Return to the freezer for another hour before enjoying.

VEGAN

BANANA *and* COCONUT ICE-CREAM

MAKES 4–6

1 large banana

1 × 400 ml tin full-fat coconut milk

This simple combination is delicious as is, or you can use it as a starting point for all kinds of fruity inventions by adding cherries, peaches, nectarines – you name it.

Simply blend the banana and coconut milk together until smooth and frothy, pour into ice-cream moulds and freeze for about 3 hours, or overnight.

BANANA, RICOTTA *and* CINNAMON

SERVES 2

1 banana, sliced lengthways

100 g drained fresh ricotta, crumbled

1 tablespoon ground cinnamon

This is a great quick snack when you crave something sweet for afternoon tea. You might want to cut out the cinnamon if you're giving it to a little one – it can cause sensitivity in babies.

Spread each banana half with ricotta and sprinkle with cinnamon.

CACAO-COATED HAZELNUTS *and* GRAPES

SERVES 6

250 g small seedless red grapes

150 g hazelnuts, skins removed

½ cup cacao butter

2 tablespoons raw cacao powder

This is a brilliant after-dinner treat, especially when served with a cheese platter for some appreciative adults. The bitterness of the cacao stands out but is cut by the smooth flavour of the hazelnuts and the poppy sweetness of the grapes. Although this recipe can be enjoyed almost straight after the cacao is set, I like to prepare it the day before to give the grapes a chance to freeze through thoroughly. They keep for a couple of months, but you'll polish them off way before then, I assure you.

Line a baking tray with baking paper. Place the grapes and hazelnuts in the freezer for 10–15 minutes.

Place the cacao butter and powder in a heatproof bowl over a saucepan of gently boiling water, making sure the bottom of the bowl doesn't touch the water. Stir gently to melt.

Remove the bowl from the heat and leave to cool for a minute, then throw in the grapes and hazelnuts. Stir to coat them thoroughly, then tip them onto the prepared tray. Place them in the freezer for about 4 hours, or until the cacao has set firm and the grapes are frozen through.

VEGAN

A PARTING WORD

I always had an inkling that making a film about sugar was going to be fraught with danger. I remember having a mini-meltdown in the edit suite a few days before we finished the cut: 'Am I seriously going to put this bloody thing out into the world? Am I insane? Am I really ready for the amount of social-media pain that is coming my way?'

But lying on the floor that day, face pressed to the carpet post-tantrum, I knew these concerns were just last-minute freak-outs from a very old mode of operating, a pattern of behaviour downloaded onto my personal hard drive from a family tree floppy disk. These voices and questions had so often taken me out and knocked me off course in the past. They had garnered their success through cunning sabotage by suffocating my current belief and conviction. But this time, while chewing the carpet and staring at the dust on the skirting board that had clearly been missed with every cleaner's visit, something descended over me; it was a knowing that there was truth in this low-sugar message. That we aren't supposed to be eating the amount of sugar that we have been. That, despite the colossal marketing budgets, the health slogans, the weight-loss shakes, the conflicting morning chat-show segments, the repeated obesity level statistics, the endless social media 'rightness', there was a simple first step and it was easier than anyone realised. We just had to start eating real foods again. Sure, we are all different and everyone may require a specific way of eating that suits their lifestyle and health, but if you look at the Mediterranean diet, the Paleo diet, the low-carb diet, the Atkins diet, the Whole30 diet . . . they all have something in common. Added sugar. A distinct lack of it.

Lowering your sugar intake is the easiest first step anyone can take towards good health. All it requires is an ability to read a label and the determination to change some patterns, or re-write the software. What 'low sugar' means to you will all depend on the wonderful word that my friend Aaron Matheson taught me: context. If you are a body builder it will mean one thing, if you are type 2 diabetic it will mean something entirely different. And this raises an interesting point.

I have recently developed a theory on humans, nutrition and opinions (especially on social media). I think no one is right or wrong when it comes to food. I think we may actually all be right in our own way. You see, when we try something and it works then it becomes very personal, we own it and so we want to share it with everyone and passionately advocate it. The problem is that another person has tried something different and due to their own context, it has worked for them. They then argue the point and a Facebook thread grows into a biblical thesis of head-butting and digital hair-pulling. Both parties are 100 per cent right in what worked for them. What we all forget is that due to all the metabolic or genetic differences, microbiome health, opioid receptor sizes or even the amount of kilometres jogged on a treadmill, food will behave differently in our bodies. We need to understand this so that we can combine our collective powers and solve this crippling health crisis as soon as possible.

So before you pay hundreds of dollars for a private nutrition session or sit down and block out a meal plan with a diet guru or even order the late-night infomercial weight-loss shake, at least try the things mentioned in this book first. It is not a diet; it is just returning to a simple and natural way of eating that will begin to heal you internally, with exterior benefits thrown in. And remember, this is not about being extreme either. I think moderation is a wonderful word, as long as you truly understand its meaning. Too many people have absolutely no idea just how much added sugar they are consuming.

Make it a priority to start reducing your highly processed refined carbohydrates, and especially focus on added sugar. Let your body reconnect with real foods again. Let them have a chat and spark up vital conversations about appetite control, let them bond and heal the overworked liver, the insulin-making pancreas machine, let their hugs and connected laughter dissolve the circulating triglycerides in your bloodstream. Your body may need assistance; you may well need to go down the medication road, you may need highly specified dietetic recommended ways of eating, but at the very least make eating real foods your baseline – your non-negotable. Deeply ingrain it so it just becomes the thing you do, like breathing, like showering, like checking to see if anyone has liked a recent social-media post.

Trust your body. Respect it. Remember it is a beautiful part of nature. Honour that knowledge and fuel it predominantly with foods that belong to the natural world – real foods.

Bibliography & Suggested Reading

BOOKS

Feltham, Sam. 2014, *Slimology: The Relatively Simple Science of Slimming*. CreateSpace Independent Publishing Platform

Lindstrom, Martin. *Buyology: Truth and Lies About Why We Buy*. Crown Publishing Group, Penguin Random House, New York

Minger, Denise. 2014, *Death By Food Pyramid*. Primal Nutrition Inc, New York

Sonnenburg, Justin and Erica. 2015, *The Good Gut*. Penguin Press, New York

Underhill, Paco. 2008. *Why We Buy: The Science of Shopping*, Simon & Schuster, New York

STUDIES

Artificial sweeteners (pp39–43)

http://www.ncbi.nlm.nih.gov/pmc/articles/PMC2892765/

Yang Q. Gain weight by "going diet?" Artificial sweeteners and the neurobiology of sugar cravings. *Yale J Biol Med*. 2010 Jun;83(2):101-8.

http://ajcn.nutrition.org/content/early/2013/01/30/ajcn.112.050997.abstract

Fagherazzi G, Vilier A, Sartorelli DS, *et al*. Consumption of artificially and sugar-sweetened beverages and incident type 2 diabetes in the Etude Epidémiologique auprès des femmes de la Mutuelle Générale de l'Education Nationale–European Prospective Investigation into Cancer and Nutrition cohort. *Am J Clin Nutr*. 2013 Mar;97(3):517-23.

Carbohydrate restriction (p53)

http://www.nutritionjrnl.com/article/S0899-9007(14)00332-3/abstract

Feinman RD, Pogozelski WK, Astrup A, *et al*. Dietary carbohydrate restriction as the first approach in diabetes management: Critical review and evidence base. *Nutrition Journal*. 2015 Jan;31(1):1-13.

Classical music and shopping (p101)

http://nicolas.gueguen.free.fr/Articles/EJSR2007.pdf

Guéguen N, Jacob C, Lourel M, et al. Effects of Background Music on Consumer's Behavior: A Field Experiment in a Open-Air Market. *European Journal of Scientific Research*. 2007;16(2):268-72.

Cravings (pp9–10)

http://www.thepermanentejournal.org/issues/2015/summer/5893-sugar.html

Bartolotto C. Does Consuming Sugar and Artificial Sweeteners Change Taste Preferences? *Perm J* 2015 Summer;19(3):81-84.

http://www.ncbi.nlm.nih.gov/pubmed/24132980

Stice E, Burger KS, Yokum S. Relative ability of fat and sugar tastes to activate reward, gustatory, and somatosensory regions. *Am J Clin Nutr*. 2013 Dec;98(6):1377-84.

Fatty liver disease in Australia

http://abs.gov.au/ausstats/abs@.nsf/Lookup/4364.0.55.005Chapter1052011-12

Obesity and Chronic Disease. 4364.0.55.005 - *Australian Health Survey: Biomedical Results for Chronic Diseases, 2011-12*. Issue published 05 August 2013.

Fructose (pp98–9; 111)

http://jama.jamanetwork.com/article.aspx?articleID=1555133

Page KA, Chan O, Arora J, *et al*. Effects of Fructose vs Glucose on Regional Cerebral Blood Flow in Brain Regions Involved With Appetite and Reward Pathways. *JAMA* 2013; 309(1):63-70

http://www.ncbi.nlm.nih.gov/pmc/articles/PMC2673878/

Stanhope KL, Schwarz JM, Keim NL, *et al*. Consuming fructose-sweetened, not glucose-sweetened, beverages increases visceral adiposity and lipids and decreases insulin sensitivity in overweight/obese humans. *J Clin Invest*. 2009 May 1;119(5):1322-1334.

Good fats (p54)

http://www.prnewswire.com/news-releases/academy-of-nutrition-and-dietetics-commends-strong-evidence-based-dietary-guidelines-report-300083129.html

Brown Rodgers A (ed). Scientific Report of the 2015 Dietary Guidelines Advisory Committee. *Health.gov*. Report first published online: February 2015.

https://doc.research-and-analytics.csfb.com/docView?language=ENG&source=ulg&format=PDF&document_id=1053247551&serialid=MFT6JQWS%2b4FvvuMDBUQ7v9g4cGa84%2fgpv8mURvaRWdQ%3d

Natella S, Divan V, Giraldo M. Fat: The New Health Paradigm. Credit Suisse AG Research Institute. 2015 Sept.

Gut-health studies (p111)

newsroom.ucla.edu/releases/
changing-gut-bacteria-through-245617

Champeau, R. Changing gut bacteria through diet affects brain function, UCLA study shows. *UCLA Newsroom*, Article first published online: 28 May 2013.

ncbi.nlm.nih.gov/pubmed?term=%22Gastroenterology%22[Jour]+AND+2013[pdat]+AND+Tillisch[author]&cmd=detailssearch

Labus JS, Hubbard CS, Bueller J, et al. Impaired emotional learning and involvement of the corticotropin-releasing factor signaling system in patients with irritable bowel syndrome. *Gastroenterology* 2013 Dec;145(6):1253-61.e1-3.

ncbi.nlm.nih.gov/pubmed/21988661

Bercik P, Park AJ, Sinclair D et al. The anxiolytic effect of Bifidobacterium longum NCC3001 involves vagal pathways for gut-brain communication. *Neurogastroenterol Motil* 2011 Dec;23(12):1132-9.

ncbi.nlm.nih.gov/pubmed?term=Proceedings+of+the+National+Academy+of+Sciences+of+the+United+States+of+America[Jour]+AND+2011[pdat]+AND+Bravo[author]&cmd=detailssearchBravo JA, Forsythe P, Chew MV, et al. Ingestion of Lactobacillus strain regulates emotional behavior and central GABA receptor expression in a mouse via the vagus nerve. *Proc Natl Acad Sci U S A*. 2011 Sep 20;108(38):16050-5.

http://edition.cnn.com/2013/05/29/health/lifework-mazmanian-bacteria/index.html?utm_source=feedburner&utm_medium=feed&utm_campaign=Feed%3A+rss%2Fcnn_health+%28RSS%3A+Health%29

Murray K. Probing the mysteries of probiotics. CNN. Article first published online: 29 May 2013.

ncbi.nlm.nih.gov/pubmed?term=%22PloS+one%22[Jour]+AND+Gut+Microbiota+in+Human+Adults+with+Type+2+Diabetes+Differs+from+Non-Diabetic+Adults&TransSchema=title

Larsen N, Vogensen FK, van den Berg FW *et al.* Gut microbiota in human adults with type 2 diabetes differs from non-diabetic adults. PLoS One. 2010 Feb 5;5(2):e9085.

http://www.ncbi.nlm.nih.gov/pmc/articles/PMC2894525/

Turnbaugh PJ, Ridaura VK, Faith JJ, *et al.* The Effect of Diet on the Human Gut Microbiome: A Metagenomic Analysis in Humanized Gnotobiotic Mice. *Sci Transl Med*. 2009 Nov 11; 1(6): 6ra14.

Meat industry greenhouse emissions (p108)

http://www.worldwatch.org/node/6294

Goodland R, Anhang J. Livestock and Climate Change: What if the key actors in climate change are...cows, pigs, and chickens? *World Watch Magazine*. 2009 Nov-Dec;22(6):10-19.

Skinny people metabolically unhealthy (p27)

http://www.ncbi.nlm.nih.gov/pubmed/22871870

Carnethon MR, De Chavez PJ, Biggs ML, *et al.* Association of weight status with mortality in adults with incident diabetes. JAMA. 2012 Aug 8;308(6):581-90.

Sugar tolerance and addiction (pp8–9)

http://www.ncbi.nlm.nih.gov/pubmed/12488799

Hajnal A, Norgren R. Repeated access to sucrose augments dopamine turnover in the nucleus accumbens. *Neuroreport*. 2002 Dec 3;13(17):2213-6.

http://www.ncbi.nlm.nih.gov/pubmed/12055324

Colantuoni C, Rada P, McCarthy J, *et al.* Evidence that intermittent, excessive sugar intake causes endogenous opioid dependence. *Obes Res*. 2002 Jun;10(6):478-88.

http://www.ncbi.nlm.nih.gov/pubmed/25484352

Mangabeira V, Garcia-Mijares M, Silva MT. Sugar withdrawal and differential reinforcement of low rate (DRL) performance in rats. *Physiol Behav*. 2015 Feb;139:468-73.

Sugar and inflammation (pp14–15)

http://ajcn.nutrition.org/content/76/1/266S.full.pdf+html?cnn=yes

Jenkins DJA, Kendall CWC, Augustin LSA, et al. Glycemic index: overview of implications in health and disease. Am J Clin Nutr 2002 July; 76(1):266S-273S.

Type 2 diabetes mortality rates

http://unric.org/en/latest-un-buzz/29521-diabetes-kills-every-6-seconds

Diabetes kills every 7 seconds. *UNRIC*. Article first published online: 14 November 2014

231

Index

First published 2016 in Macmillan
by Pan Macmillan Australia Pty Ltd
1 Market Street, Sydney, New South Wales, Australia, 2000

Cataloguing-in-Publication entry is available
from the National Library of Australia http://catalogue.nla.gov.au

Design by Trisha Garner, DesignPatsy
Illustrations by Alice Oehr
Food styling by Michelle Noerianto
(except pp 35; 46; 114; 116; 118; and produce shots by
Deborah Kaloper)
Food preparation by Kerrie Ray
(except pp 35; 46; 114; 116; 118; and produce shots by Emma Warren)
Index by Glenda Browne
Typeset in Archer Book 10.5/14.5 by Post Pre-Press Group
Colour and reproduction by Splitting Image Colour Studio
Printed in China

Acknowledgements

We would like to acknowledge all the support we have had over the past year. We are constantly humbled by listening to people's transformational stories, whether via social media or a quick chat in the street. We strongly believe that we are all in this together. Your support has driven us to continue spreading the real-food message. We are very grateful.

Thank you to Rob Palmer, Michelle Noerianto and Kerrie Ray for doing a fantastic job of the food photography, styling and preparation. Thank you to Pino's Fine Food and Gary's Quality Meats at Prahran Market, Melbourne. Also to OzHarvest (ozharvest.org) who collected the produce used in the photoshoot.

Thank you to the team at Pan Macmillan: Ingrid Ohlsson, Trisha Garner, Ariane Durkin, Sally Devenish, Jodi De Vantier, Charlotte Ree, Naomi van Groll, Helena Holmgren, Rebecca Hamilton, Tara Goedjen and Megan Ellis.

About the authors

Damon Gameau released his first feature film, *That Sugar Film*, in 2015. It went on to become the highest-grossing Australian documentary of all time across Australia and New Zealand. The film has also picked up a host of awards around the world, including the AACTA award (the 'Aussie Oscars') for Best Documentary. The accompanying book, *That Sugar Book*, became a bestseller and has since been published in more than 15 countries and eight languages around the world. Damon has a passion for health, especially helping the next generation to understand the importance of eating well.

Zoe Tuckwell-Smith has enjoyed a successful career in the entertainment industry for more than 12 years. Working closely behind the scenes with Damon on *That Sugar Film* – and then witnessing how the message resonated with the audience – inspired her to help people find practical ways to make positive changes to their health. This is Zoe's first foray into recipe writing. She and Damon live in the Dandenong Ranges, Victoria, with their daughter, Velvet.